HowExpert Guide to Cross Country Running

101 Tips to Learn How to Run Cross Country, Build Endurance, Improve Nutrition, Prevent Injuries, and Compete in Cross Country Races

HowExpert with Elliot Redcay

For more tips related to this topic, visit HowExpert.com/crosscountry.

Recommended Resources

- HowExpert.com – How To Guides on All Topics from A to Z by Everyday Experts.
- HowExpert.com/free – Free HowExpert Email Newsletter.
- HowExpert.com/books – HowExpert Books
- HowExpert.com/courses – HowExpert Courses
- HowExpert.com/clothing – HowExpert Clothing
- HowExpert.com/membership – HowExpert Membership Site
- HowExpert.com/affiliates – HowExpert Affiliate Program
- HowExpert.com/jobs – HowExpert Jobs
- HowExpert.com/writers – Write About Your #1 Passion/Knowledge/Expertise & Become a HowExpert Author.
- HowExpert.com/resources – Additional HowExpert Recommended Resources
- YouTube.com/HowExpert – Subscribe to HowExpert YouTube.
- Instagram.com/HowExpert – Follow HowExpert on Instagram.
- Facebook.com/HowExpert – Follow HowExpert on Facebook.
- TikTok.com/@HowExpert – Follow HowExpert on TikTok.

Publisher's Foreword

Dear HowExpert Reader,

HowExpert publishes quick 'how to' guides on all topics from A to Z by everyday experts.

At HowExpert, our mission is to discover, empower, and maximize everyday people's talents to ultimately make a positive impact in the world for all topics from A to Z...one everyday expert at a time!

All of our HowExpert guides are written by everyday people just like you and me, who have a passion, knowledge, and expertise for a specific topic.

We take great pride in selecting everyday experts who have a passion, real-life experience in a topic, and excellent writing skills to teach you about the topic you are also passionate about and eager to learn.

We hope you get a lot of value from our HowExpert guides, and it can make a positive impact on your life in some way. All of our readers, including you, help us continue living our mission of positively impacting the world for all spheres of influences from A to Z.

If you enjoyed one of our HowExpert guides, then please take a moment to send us your feedback from wherever you got this book.

Thank you, and we wish you all the best in all aspects of life.

Sincerely,

Byungjoon "BJ" Min / 민병준
Founder & Publisher of HowExpert
HowExpert.com

PS...If you are also interested in becoming a HowExpert author, then please visit our website at HowExpert.com/writers. Thank you & again, all the best! John 3:16

Table of Contents

Chapter 1: Introduction

Getting Started With Cross Country Running

Tip 1: Find your "why" for cross country running.

Cross country running is a physically and mentally demanding sport that requires a lot of dedication and hard work. As such, it is important to find your "why" for running cross country before you start training. Your "why" is your personal reason or motivation for running that will keep you focused and motivated throughout your training.

For some runners, their "why" may be to improve their overall health and fitness, while others may be motivated by competition and the desire to win races. Regardless of your reason, it is important to identify it early on and use it as a driving force throughout your training.

To find your "why" for cross country running, start by asking yourself what motivates you to run. Is it the challenge of pushing yourself to your limits? Is it the feeling of accomplishment you get after completing a long run or race? Is it the social aspect of being part of a team or a running club?

Once you have identified your motivation, make it a point to remind yourself of it regularly. Write it down in a journal, post it on your fridge or bathroom mirror, or even make it the background on your phone or computer. This constant reminder will help you stay focused and committed to your training, even when it gets tough.

In addition to keeping you motivated, finding your "why" can also help you set specific goals for your training. For example, if your "why" is to improve your overall health and fitness, you may set a goal to run a certain distance or time each week. If your "why" is competition, you may set a goal to finish in a certain place or time in a race.

In conclusion, finding your "why" is an essential first step in your cross country running journey. It will provide you with the motivation and focus you need to achieve your goals and become a successful cross country runner.

Tip 2: Understand the benefits of cross country running.

Cross country running is a sport that involves running on natural terrains such as hills, grass, dirt, and gravel. It is a physically and mentally demanding sport that requires endurance, strength, and mental toughness. In addition to being a fun and challenging sport, cross country running also has many benefits for your physical and mental health.

One of the main benefits of cross country running is that it is an excellent form of cardiovascular exercise. Running long distances at a moderate to high intensity increases your heart rate, strengthens your heart and lungs, and improves your overall cardiovascular health. It also helps to lower your blood pressure, reduce your risk of heart disease, and improve your blood sugar control.

Another benefit of cross country running is that it helps to strengthen your lower body muscles. Running on uneven terrain, uphill and downhill, engages muscles in your legs, hips, and core that are not typically used in other forms of exercise. This helps to improve your balance, stability, and overall strength.

Cross country running is also a great way to relieve stress and improve mental health. Running releases endorphins, natural chemicals that help reduce stress and improve mood. It can also provide a sense of accomplishment and boost your confidence and self-esteem.

Additionally, cross country running can be a social activity that fosters teamwork and camaraderie. Joining a cross country team or running club can provide a supportive and motivating environment that helps you stay committed to your training and achieve your goals.

In conclusion, cross country running is a challenging and rewarding sport that has numerous benefits for your physical and mental health. It can improve your cardiovascular health, strengthen your muscles, reduce stress, and provide a supportive social environment. Whether you are a beginner or an experienced runner, cross country running is a great way to improve your overall health and fitness.

Tip 3: Scope out the area before you start running.

Before starting your cross country run, it is important to take the time to scope out the area and assess any potential hazards or obstacles. By doing so, you can ensure that you have a safe and enjoyable running experience.

One of the first things to consider when scoping out the area is the terrain. Cross country running typically involves running on natural terrains such as hills, dirt paths, and rocky trails. Take a few minutes to survey the terrain and look for any potential hazards, such as loose rocks, tree roots, or steep drops. This will help you to adjust your pace and footwork accordingly to avoid tripping or falling.

Another important factor to consider when scoping out the area is the weather. Check the weather forecast for the day and dress appropriately for the conditions. If it is hot and sunny, make sure to bring sunscreen and plenty of water to stay hydrated. If it is cold and rainy, wear appropriate clothing to stay warm and dry.

In addition, it is also important to be aware of any potential safety concerns in the area. For example, if you are running in a remote area or unfamiliar terrain, it is a good idea to bring a phone and let someone know where you will be running and how long you expect to be gone. If you are running in an urban area, be aware of traffic and crosswalks to ensure that you can safely navigate busy streets.

Finally, take the time to warm up and stretch before starting your run. This can help to prevent injury and prepare your body for the physical demands of cross country running.

In conclusion, scoping out the area before starting your cross country run can help you to identify potential hazards, adjust your pace and footwork, and stay safe and comfortable during your run. By taking the time to assess the terrain, weather, and safety concerns, you can ensure that you have a successful and enjoyable running experience.

Tip 4: Figure out where all the bathrooms are in your area.

It is important to know where the bathrooms are located in your area before embarking on a cross country run. This can help you plan your route and avoid any discomfort or embarrassment while on the run.

To find the bathrooms in your area, start by checking online maps and directories for public restrooms in local parks or recreational areas. If you are a member of a gym or fitness center, check their website or inquire with staff to see if they have available facilities.

Another option is to ask local businesses such as coffee shops, restaurants, or gas stations if public restrooms are available. Many public libraries and community centers also have public restrooms that may be available for use during regular business hours.

In addition, if you are running in a residential area, it may be possible to find public restrooms at local schools, community centers, or churches. Be sure to check with the appropriate authorities before entering any private property.

It is also a good idea to carry some emergency supplies with you on your runs, such as toilet paper, hand sanitizer, and a plastic bag for waste disposal in case you cannot find a restroom in time.

Overall, knowing where the bathrooms are located in your area can help you plan your cross country run more effectively and avoid any potential discomfort or embarrassment. By utilizing online resources, asking local businesses, and checking public facilities, you can ensure that you are prepared for any unexpected bathroom needs while on the run.

Learn the benefits of Cross Country Running

Tip 5: Running longer distances in cross country can improve your endurance and stamina.

Yes, running longer distances in cross country can certainly help to improve your endurance and stamina. Endurance is the ability of your body to sustain physical activity for an extended period of time, while stamina refers to the amount of energy you can exert for an extended period of time.

When you run longer distances in cross country, your body is forced to adapt and become more efficient at using oxygen to produce energy. This process, known as aerobic conditioning, helps to improve your endurance by increasing your body's ability to transport and utilize oxygen during exercise. Over time, this adaptation can lead to improved cardiovascular fitness, decreased fatigue, and increased energy levels.

In addition to improving your endurance, running longer distances in cross country can also help to improve your stamina by increasing the amount of glycogen stored in your muscles. Glycogen is a form of energy stored in your muscles and liver and is used during physical activity. By increasing your muscle glycogen stores through longer runs, you can improve your body's ability to maintain energy levels during prolonged exercise.

Furthermore, running longer distances can also help to improve your mental stamina by increasing your tolerance for discomfort and challenging situations. This mental resilience can translate to other areas of your life, helping you better cope with stress and adversity.

It is important to note that increasing your mileage too quickly can increase your risk of injury. It is recommended to gradually increase your distance and intensity over time to avoid overuse injuries and allow your body to adapt properly.

In conclusion, running longer distances in cross country can be an effective way to improve your endurance and stamina. Through aerobic conditioning, increased glycogen storage, and improved mental resilience, longer runs can help you become a stronger and more efficient runner. However, it is important to gradually increase your mileage to avoid injury and allow your body to adapt properly.

Tip 6: Running on natural terrain can strengthen your leg muscles and core.

Cross country running is a sport that involves running on natural terrains such as hills, dirt paths, and rocky trails. This type of terrain can provide a unique and challenging workout that can help to strengthen your leg muscles and core.

When running on natural terrain, your body is required to adjust to the changing terrain, which can help activate more muscles than running on a flat surface. In addition, the uneven surface can help to improve balance and stability, which can, in turn, strengthen the core muscles. The core muscles include the abdominals, obliques, and lower back muscles, which are essential for maintaining good posture and stability during running.

In addition, running on natural terrain can also help to strengthen the leg muscles. Hills and rough terrain require the muscles in your legs to work harder to push off and maintain balance. This increased effort can help to strengthen the quadriceps, hamstrings, calves, and glutes.

By regularly incorporating natural terrain into your cross country training, you can continue to challenge your leg muscles and core and build overall strength and endurance. It is important to start slowly and gradually increase the intensity and duration of your runs as you build strength and endurance. Additionally, stretching before and after your run can help to prevent injury and aid in recovery.

Overall, running on natural terrain can provide a challenging and rewarding workout that can help to strengthen your leg muscles and core. By incorporating natural terrain into your cross country training, you can improve your overall strength and endurance and achieve your running goals.

Tip 7: Learn basic nutrition science.

Nutrition science is the study of how food affects the body and the mechanisms behind the relationship between diet and health. Learning the basics of nutrition science can help you make informed decisions about your diet and improve your overall health.

One key aspect of nutrition science is understanding the three macronutrients: carbohydrates, proteins, and fats. Carbohydrates provide energy and are found in foods such as bread, pasta, and fruits. Proteins are essential for building and repairing tissues and can be found in foods such as meat, fish, and beans. Fats provide energy and help support brain function and can be found in foods such as nuts, seeds, and oils.

Another important aspect of nutrition science is understanding micronutrients such as vitamins and minerals. These nutrients are essential for overall health and play a variety of roles in the body, such as supporting the immune system and aiding in the production of hormones.

It is also important to understand the concept of calories and how they relate to weight management. A calorie is a unit of energy, and consuming more calories than your body needs can lead to weight gain. Conversely, consuming fewer calories than your body needs can lead to weight loss.

Finally, it is important to understand the role of hydration in nutrition science. Water is essential for overall health and helps to regulate body temperature, transport nutrients throughout the body, and remove waste. Therefore, it is recommended that adults drink at least eight cups of water per day.

Overall, learning the basics of nutrition science can help you make informed decisions about your diet and improve your overall health. By understanding the macronutrients, micronutrients, calories, and hydration, you can make choices that support your health and well-being.

Tip 8: Learn how cross country running can reduce stress and anxiety.

Cross country running can be a great way to reduce stress and anxiety. Running, in general, has been shown to have a positive impact on mental health, and cross country running offers additional benefits due to the natural environment in which it takes place.

When running, the body releases endorphins, natural chemicals that can help to improve mood and reduce stress. These chemicals can help to reduce feelings of anxiety and depression, leaving you feeling more relaxed and energized. Additionally, running can help improve sleep quality, which can have a positive impact on overall mental health.

Cross country running offers additional benefits because it takes place in natural settings such as parks or forests. Research has shown that spending time in nature can help to reduce stress and anxiety and improve mood. In addition, the natural environment can provide a sense of calm and relaxation, which can enhance the positive effects of running on mental health.

Cross country running can also offer a sense of accomplishment and a boost in self-confidence. Completing a challenging run on uneven terrain can give you a sense of achievement and help improve self-esteem, which can have a positive impact on mental health.

It is important to note that while cross country running can be a great way to reduce stress and anxiety, it is not a replacement for professional mental health care. Therefore, if you are experiencing persistent feelings of anxiety or depression, it is important to seek the help of a qualified mental health professional.

Overall, cross country running can be a great way to reduce stress and anxiety and improve overall mental health. In addition, the combination of physical activity and exposure to nature can provide a sense of calm and relaxation, leaving you feeling energized and refreshed.

How to Stay Motivated Throughout Your Training

Tip 9: Set specific, measurable goals to help you stay motivated and track your progress.

By setting clear goals, you can stay motivated and focused on your progress, which can help you to reach your full potential as a runner.

When setting goals, it is important to make them specific and measurable. This means that they should be clearly defined and able to be tracked over time. For example, instead of setting a goal to "run more," you could set a specific goal to "run three miles three times per week." This goal is specific, measurable, and can be tracked over time to see if you are making progress.

Setting specific, measurable goals can help you to stay motivated by giving you a sense of accomplishment as you work towards achieving them. When you reach a goal, you can celebrate your progress and use that momentum to push yourself even further. Additionally, by tracking your progress over time, you can see the improvements you are making, which can be a great source of motivation to continue working towards your goals.

When setting goals, it is important to make them realistic and achievable. Setting goals that are too difficult or unrealistic can be demotivating and may lead to feelings of failure or disappointment. Instead, set goals that are challenging but achievable and adjust them as needed based on your progress.

Overall, setting specific, measurable goals can be a powerful tool in achieving success in cross country running. By staying focused on your goals and tracking your progress, you can stay motivated and achieve your full potential as a runner.

Tip 10: Find a running partner that can make your training more enjoyable and hold you accountable.

Finding a running partner can be a great way to make your cross country training more enjoyable and hold yourself accountable to your goals. In addition, running with a partner can provide a sense of motivation, support, and companionship that can help you to stay committed to your training.

One of the benefits of having a running partner is the ability to share your training experience with someone else. Running can be a solitary activity, and having someone to talk to while you train can make the experience more enjoyable. Additionally, a running partner can provide encouragement and motivation during difficult runs, helping you to push through when you might otherwise give up.

Having a running partner can also help hold you accountable for your training goals. When you have someone else relying on you to show up for a run, you are more likely to stay committed to your training schedule. Additionally, a running partner can provide a sense of competition that can help you to push yourself further and achieve more than you might on your own.

When looking for a running partner, consider someone with similar fitness goals and experience level as you. It can also be helpful to find someone whose schedule and availability align with yours, making it easier to train together consistently.

Overall, finding a running partner can be a great way to make your cross country training more enjoyable and hold yourself accountable to your goals. With a supportive and motivated partner by your side, you can push yourself further and achieve more than you might on your own.

Tip 11: Think about joining a running group that can provide you with additional motivation and support.

Joining a running group can be a great way to boost your motivation, find support, and improve your cross country running skills. Running groups can provide a sense of camaraderie and accountability that can help you to stay committed to your training goals and push yourself further as a runner.

One of the benefits of joining a running group is the ability to train with like-minded individuals who share your passion for running. You can find a group that aligns with your fitness level, experience, and goals and receive guidance and support from experienced runners or coaches. In addition, running groups often offer structured training plans, group workouts, and opportunities for cross-training and injury prevention, which can help you to improve your overall fitness and performance.

Being part of a running group can also provide a sense of motivation and accountability that can help you to stay committed to your training goals. You can share your progress with your group members, celebrate each other's achievements, and push each other to keep going when training gets tough. Additionally, running with a group can make training more enjoyable and social, which can help to alleviate the boredom and monotony that can come with solo training.

When looking for a running group, consider factors such as location, schedule, and the type of training offered. Look for a group that is welcoming and supportive and that aligns with your training needs and goals. Additionally, make sure to communicate with the group leaders or coaches about any injuries or health concerns you may have, and make sure to prioritize your safety and well-being during training.

Overall, joining a running group can be a great way to find additional motivation and support as you work towards your cross country running goals. With the guidance and encouragement of experienced runners and the support of a community, you can take your running to the next level and achieve more than you ever thought possible.

Tip 12: Mix up your training to prevent boredom and help you stay motivated.

Mixing up your training is a great way to prevent boredom and stay motivated during your cross country training. When you perform the same workouts day after day, it can become monotonous and tedious, leading to a lack of motivation and even burnout. By adding variety to your training routine, you can keep things fresh and exciting, challenge your body in new ways, and prevent boredom and plateauing.

One way to mix up your training is by varying your running terrain. Instead of always running on the same surface, try running on different types of terrain, such as trails, hills, or even the beach.

This can help improve your balance, coordination, and overall strength, while also providing a new and interesting training environment.

Another way to mix up your training is by incorporating different types of workouts into your routine. For example, you might try interval training, tempo runs, hill repeats, or fartlek, all of which can help to improve your speed, endurance, and overall fitness. You might also consider incorporating cross-training activities, such as swimming, cycling, or yoga, which can help to improve your overall fitness and prevent injury.

Finally, consider incorporating social activities into your training routine. This might involve running with a group, participating in a local race, or even signing up for a cross country training camp or retreat. These activities can help provide a sense of community and support while also adding an element of fun and excitement to your training.

Overall, mixing up your training is a great way to prevent boredom, stay motivated, and improve your cross country running skills. By varying your terrain, workouts, and social activities, you can keep things interesting and challenging while also preventing injury and achieving your training goals.

Tip 13: Reward yourself for achieving training goals to help you feel accomplished.

Rewarding yourself for achieving training goals can be a powerful motivator and help you feel accomplished as you progress toward your cross country running goals. Setting specific training goals, such as running a certain distance or time, can help you to stay focused and motivated during training. And when you achieve those goals, taking the time to reward yourself can help to reinforce positive behavior and keep you moving forward.

When it comes to rewarding yourself, it's important to choose rewards that are meaningful and aligned with your values and goals. This might include treating yourself to a new piece of running gear, taking a relaxing bath, or indulging in your favorite healthy snack. The key is choosing rewards that will help you feel accomplished and motivated while supporting your overall health and well-being.

It's also important to set clear guidelines for when and how you will reward yourself. For example, you might choose to reward yourself after achieving a specific training goal, such as running a certain distance or completing a challenging workout. You might also consider setting specific criteria for when you will allow yourself to indulge in certain rewards, such as limiting your treat to once a week or only after a particularly challenging workout.

Finally, remember to celebrate your accomplishments and give yourself credit for your hard work and dedication. Celebrating your successes, no matter how small, can help to boost your confidence and reinforce positive behavior, helping you to stay motivated and committed to your cross country running goals.

In conclusion, rewarding yourself for achieving training goals can be a powerful motivator and help you feel accomplished during your cross country training. By setting clear goals, choosing meaningful rewards, and celebrating your successes, you can stay focused and motivated, and achieve your running goals with greater ease and satisfaction.

Tip 14: Focus on the long-term benefits of cross country running to help you stay motivated.

When it comes to staying motivated during your cross country running training, it can be helpful to focus on the long-term benefits that this form of exercise can provide. While it's natural to want to see immediate results and improvements, it's important to remember that the benefits of cross country running often extend far beyond the short term. By keeping your eyes on the prize and focusing on the long-term benefits, you can stay motivated and committed to your training goals.

One of the most significant long-term benefits of cross country running is improved cardiovascular health. Regular running can help to strengthen your heart and lungs, reduce your risk of heart disease and other chronic illnesses, and improve your overall endurance and stamina. Additionally, regular running can help to reduce stress and anxiety, boost your mood and mental health, and promote better sleep.

Another long-term benefit of cross country running is improved physical fitness and body composition. Running can help to build lean muscle mass, improve your overall strength and endurance, and burn calories and fat. Over time, this can lead to a leaner, more toned physique and improved overall health and well-being.

Finally, cross country running can provide a sense of accomplishment and personal satisfaction that can help to improve your confidence and self-esteem. Achieving your training goals, competing in races, and seeing the progress you've made over time can be incredibly rewarding and empowering, helping you feel more confident and capable in other areas of your life.

In summary, by focusing on the long-term benefits of cross country running, such as improved cardiovascular health, physical fitness, and personal satisfaction, you can stay motivated and committed to your training goals. Remembering the big picture can help you push through challenging workouts, stay consistent with your training, and achieve your running goals with greater ease and enjoyment.

Tip 15: Visualize success and the feeling of accomplishment to help you stay motivated throughout your training.

Visualization is a powerful tool that can help you stay motivated and focused during your cross country running training. By picturing yourself achieving your goals and feeling a sense of accomplishment, you can tap into the power of your mind to help you stay on track and push through challenging workouts.

To start using visualization as a motivational tool:

1. Take some time each day to picture yourself achieving your training goals.
2. Close your eyes and imagine yourself running with ease and confidence, feeling strong and energized.
3. Picture yourself crossing the finish line of a race, feeling a sense of pride and accomplishment.
4. Visualize the feeling of success and the positive impact your running can have on your life.

In addition to visualization, it can be helpful to create a vision board or other visual representation of your goals. This might include pictures of runners or races that inspire you, motivational quotes or mantras, or other images that represent the success and accomplishment you hope to achieve through your training. Display this vision board in a prominent place where you will see it frequently, such as on your bedroom wall or in your training area.

Finally, remember to use positive self-talk to reinforce your motivation and confidence. Instead of focusing on negative thoughts or self-doubt, use positive affirmations and statements to encourage yourself and boost your confidence. Remind yourself of your strengths and accomplishments, and believe in your ability to achieve your goals.

In conclusion, visualization is a powerful tool that can help you stay motivated and focused during your cross country running training. By picturing yourself achieving your goals and feeling a sense of accomplishment, you can tap into the power of your mind to help you stay on track and push through challenging workouts. By combining visualization with positive self-talk and a clear vision of your goals, you can achieve your running goals with greater ease and enjoyment.

Chapter Review

- Find your "why" for cross country running - understand the benefits of cross country running and identify what motivates you to train and compete.
- Use visualization to stay motivated and focused during your training - picture yourself achieving your goals, create a vision board, and use positive self-talk to reinforce your motivation and confidence.
- Set specific, measurable goals and track your progress - this helps you stay motivated and hold yourself accountable for your training.
- Mix up your training and find a running partner or group to prevent boredom and provide additional motivation and support.
- Reward yourself for achieving training goals - this helps you feel accomplished and motivated to continue working towards your goals.

Chapter 2: Building Your Endurance

Importance of a Solid Foundation in Cross Country Running

Tip 16: Start with a base mileage.

One of the most important tips for anyone looking to start cross country running is to establish a solid base mileage. Your base mileage is the amount of running you can comfortably handle without getting injured or feeling overly fatigued. The idea is to gradually increase this mileage over time, allowing your body to adapt and become stronger.

When starting out, it's important to be realistic about your current fitness level and build up your mileage gradually. If you're new to running, you may want to start with just a few miles a week and gradually increase by 10-20% each week. Then, as your body adapts, you can gradually increase your mileage until you're running five or six days a week.

One key thing to keep in mind is that your base mileage should be done at a comfortable pace. For example, you should be able to carry on a conversation without feeling out of breath or struggling to keep up. This will help you build endurance and strengthen your cardiovascular system without putting too much stress on your body.

It's also important to remember that everyone's base mileage will be different. Some runners may be able to handle more mileage than others, depending on factors such as age, fitness level, and previous running experience. So don't compare yourself to others – focus on building a base that works for you.

In summary, starting with a base mileage is crucial for anyone looking to start cross country running. Gradually building up your mileage and running at a comfortable pace will help you avoid injury and build endurance. Remember to be patient, listen to your body, and enjoy the process of becoming a stronger and fitter runner.

Tip 17: Gradually increase your mileage.

Gradually increasing your mileage is an essential part of becoming a successful cross country runner. However, it's important to do so in a safe and sustainable way.

When increasing your mileage, it's recommended that you do so by no more than 10-20% each week. This will allow your body to adapt to the increased stress and prevent injuries. It's also a good idea to include a recovery week every 3-4 weeks, during which you decrease your mileage and allow your body to recover and rebuild.

It's important to listen to your body and not push yourself too hard. If you feel excessively fatigued or notice any pain or discomfort, it's important to take a step back and rest. Cross-training, such as swimming or cycling, can also help you maintain fitness while giving your body a break from the impact of running.

In addition to increasing your mileage gradually, it's also important to incorporate variety into your training. This can include different types of workouts, such as intervals or hill repeats, and different types of terrain, such as trails or grass. This will help prevent boredom and challenge your body in different ways, leading to better overall fitness and performance.

In summary, gradually increasing your mileage is a key part of becoming a successful cross country runner, but it's important to do so in a safe and sustainable way. Listen to your body, incorporate variety into your training, and enjoy the process of becoming a stronger and fitter runner.

Tip 18: Listen to your body.

Listening to your body is an important aspect of cross country running. It involves paying attention to how your body feels during and after a run and adjusting your training accordingly.

One of the most common signs that you need to listen to your body is fatigue. If you feel excessively tired, it's important to take a break or reduce your training volume. Overtraining can lead to injuries, burnout, and decreased performance.

Pain is another sign that you need to listen to your body. If you experience pain during or after a run, it's important to address it promptly. Ignoring pain can lead to more serious injuries that can set you back in your training.

In addition to fatigue and pain, other signs that you need to listen to your body include poor sleep, changes in appetite, and changes in mood or motivation. These can all be indicators that your body needs rest or a change in your training routine.

It's important to note that listening to your body doesn't mean giving up at the first sign of discomfort. Running can be challenging, and it's natural to experience some discomfort or fatigue. However, if you're constantly feeling unwell or unable to recover from your workouts, it's important to make adjustments to your training.

In summary, listening to your body is an important aspect of cross country running. Paying attention to signs of fatigue, pain, and other changes in your body can help you avoid injury, burnout, and other setbacks. It's important to strike a balance between challenging yourself and taking care of your body and to make adjustments to your training as needed.

Tip 19: Rest and recovery.

Rest and recovery are crucial aspects of cross country running. In fact, they are just as important as training itself. Giving your body time to recover after workouts allow it to repair and rebuild, leading to improved performance and decreased risk of injury.

One of the most important aspects of rest and recovery is getting enough sleep. Sleep is when your body does the majority of its repair work, so it's important to prioritize getting enough restful sleep each night. Most adults need 7-9 hours of sleep per night, although this can vary from person to person.

Another important aspect of rest and recovery is taking rest days. Rest days give your body a break from the impact of running and allow it to recover from the stress of training. Rest days can also help prevent burnout and keep you motivated to continue training.

In addition to rest days, active recovery can also be beneficial. This can include low-impact activities such as yoga, stretching, or foam rolling. These activities can help improve circulation, reduce soreness, and prevent stiffness.

Finally, proper nutrition and hydration are important for rest and recovery. Eating a balanced diet that includes plenty of fruits, vegetables, whole grains, and lean protein can help support recovery. Staying hydrated by drinking enough water throughout the day is also crucial.

In summary, rest and recovery are essential aspects of cross country running. Getting enough sleep, taking rest days, engaging in active recovery, and eating a healthy diet can all help support recovery and improve performance. In addition, by taking care of your body during rest and recovery, you'll be better able to handle the demands of training and reach your running goals.

Tip 20: Incorporate cross-training.

Incorporating cross-training into your cross country running routine can be a great way to improve your overall fitness and prevent injury. Cross-training involves activities other than running that can help you build strength, flexibility, and endurance.

One of the most popular cross-training activities for runners is cycling. Cycling is a low-impact activity that can help build cardiovascular fitness and strengthen the muscles in your legs without putting as much stress on your joints as running.

Swimming is another excellent cross-training activity for runners. Swimming is a full-body workout that can help build endurance, improve lung capacity, and increase cardiovascular fitness. Additionally, swimming is a low-impact activity that can be particularly beneficial for runners who are recovering from injuries.

Strength training is also an important component of cross-training for runners. Building strength in your legs, core, and upper body can help improve your running form, prevent injury, and increase your overall performance. Strength training can include exercises such as squats, lunges, planks, and push-ups.

Yoga and Pilates are also great cross-training activities for runners. These activities can help improve flexibility, balance, and core strength, which are important for running. Additionally, yoga and Pilates can help reduce stress and improve mental focus, which can benefit your overall running performance.

Incorporating cross-training into your cross country running routine doesn't mean you have to give up running altogether. Rather, it's about finding activities that complement and support your running goals. By incorporating cross-training activities into your routine, you'll improve your overall fitness, prevent injury, and become a stronger and more well-rounded runner.

Tip 21: Build a strong foundation before increasing intensity.

Building a strong foundation before increasing intensity is a key principle of effective cross country running training. This means that before you start focusing on speed, interval training, or other high-intensity workouts, you need to first establish a base level of fitness and endurance.

One of the best ways to build a strong foundation is to focus on increasing your mileage gradually over time. Start with a comfortable distance that you can run without feeling overly fatigued, and then gradually increase the distance each week. This will help your body adapt to the demands of running and improve your cardiovascular fitness.

In addition to gradually increasing your mileage, it's important to focus on developing good running form and technique. This can include maintaining an upright posture, landing softly on your feet, and keeping your arms and shoulders relaxed. Good running form can help reduce the risk of injury and improve your overall efficiency as a runner.

Strength training can also be beneficial for building a strong foundation. Focusing on exercises that target the muscles used in running, such as the glutes, hips, and core, can help improve your overall strength and stability as a runner. This can help you maintain good form and reduce the risk of injury as you increase your training intensity.

Finally, it's important to give your body time to rest and recover. Incorporating rest days into your training plan can help prevent burnout and allow your body to recover from the stress of running. Active recovery activities such as yoga, stretching, or foam rolling can also be beneficial for improving recovery and reducing soreness.

By focusing on building a strong foundation before increasing intensity, you'll be better prepared to handle the demands of more intense workouts and improve your overall performance as a cross country runner.

Long Runs and Easy Runs

Tip 22: Incorporate long runs into your training.

Incorporating long runs into your cross country running training is a crucial aspect of building endurance and preparing your body for longer-distance races. Long runs can also help you develop mental toughness and confidence in your ability to complete challenging distances.

A long run is typically defined as a run longer than your typical daily or weekly mileage. For example, if you typically run 3-4 miles per day, a long run might be 6-8 miles or more. It's important to gradually build up your long run distance over time, adding no more than 10% of your total mileage each week to avoid overtraining and injury.

One of the benefits of long runs is that they help improve your cardiovascular fitness and endurance. By challenging yourself to run longer distances, you'll train your body to become more efficient at using oxygen and nutrients to power your muscles. This can lead to improvements in your overall running speed and performance.

Long runs can also be mentally challenging, as they require focus and determination to complete. By pushing yourself to complete longer distances, you'll develop mental toughness and resilience that can help you during races and other challenging situations.

It's important to remember that long runs are not about speed or performance. Rather, they are about building endurance and developing a strong fitness base. Therefore, running at a comfortable pace that allows you to complete the distance without feeling overly fatigued is important.

Incorporating long runs into your cross country running training can help you build endurance, improve your overall fitness, and develop mental toughness. By gradually increasing your long run distance and focusing on proper pacing and technique, you'll be

better prepared to tackle longer-distance races and achieve your
running goals.

Tip 23: Increase your long run distance gradually.

Increasing your long run distance gradually is essential to avoid
injury and overtraining while building your endurance and
preparing your body for longer distances. Adding too much distance
too quickly can cause stress on your body, leading to fatigue and
injury. Here are some tips on how to increase your long run
distance safely:

1. Increase distance by no more than 10% per week: A general
    guideline for safely increasing long run distance is to add no
    more than 10% of your total weekly mileage each week. This
    allows your body to gradually adapt to the new distance and
    minimizes the risk of injury.
2. Take a step back every third week: After increasing your long
    run distance for two weeks, take a step back in distance every
    third week. This will give your body a chance to recover and
    adapt to the increased workload.
3. Listen to your body: Pay attention to how your body is
    feeling during and after your long runs. If you are
    experiencing pain or fatigue, it may be a sign that you need
    to slow down or take a break.
4. Incorporate rest days: Make sure to give your body time to
    recover by incorporating rest days into your training plan.
    This will help prevent burnout and reduce the risk of injury.
5. Fuel and hydrate properly: Make sure to fuel your body
    properly before, during, and after your long runs. This
    includes staying hydrated and consuming enough
    carbohydrates to maintain energy levels.

By gradually increasing your long run distance, you'll be able to
safely build your endurance and prepare your body for longer
distances. Remember to listen to your body, take rest days, and fuel

properly to maximize your performance and reduce the risk of injury.

Tip 24: Use easy runs for recovery.

Easy runs can be an effective tool for recovery in your cross country running training. Recovery is a critical aspect of any training plan, as it allows your body to repair and rebuild after workouts and races. Easy runs can help facilitate this recovery by promoting blood flow and reducing muscle soreness and inflammation.

An easy run is typically a shorter run done at a slower pace than your typical workout or race pace. The goal of an easy run is to promote recovery and allow your body to adapt to the stresses of training without adding additional stress.

When incorporating easy runs into your training plan, it's important to listen to your body and adjust your pace and distance as needed. If you're feeling fatigued or sore, it may be beneficial to reduce the distance or intensity of your easy run. On the other hand, if you're feeling good, you can add a bit more distance or pick up the pace slightly.

In addition to promoting recovery, easy runs can also provide mental and emotional benefits. Running at an easy pace can be a relaxing and enjoyable way to clear your mind and reduce stress. It can also provide an opportunity to enjoy the outdoors and appreciate the scenery.

Overall, incorporating easy runs into your cross country running training can be an effective way to promote recovery and improve overall performance. By listening to your body, adjusting your pace and distance as needed, and making sure to fuel and hydrate properly, you'll be able to maximize the benefits of easy runs and achieve your running goals.

Tip 25: Keep your easy runs at a conversational pace.

It's important to keep your pace at a conversational level to maximize the benefits of easy runs for recovery. This means running at a pace that allows you to comfortably hold a conversation while running.

Running at a conversational pace has several benefits. First, it helps to reduce the stress on your body, as you're not pushing your heart rate or breathing to its maximum levels. This allows your body to recover more efficiently from previous workouts and prepare for upcoming ones.

In addition, running at a conversational pace can help improve your aerobic fitness, as it encourages the development of the aerobic system and strengthens the heart and lungs. It can also help you maintain a healthy body composition by burning fat for energy, which is more efficient at lower intensities.

Furthermore, running at a conversational pace can be mentally and emotionally beneficial, as it allows you to enjoy the run and take in your surroundings. It can be a refreshing change from the more intense workouts and races in your training plan.

It's helpful to monitor your breathing and heart rate to ensure that your easy runs are at a conversational pace. If you find yourself out of breath or struggling to speak, slow down your pace until you can comfortably hold a conversation.

Overall, keeping your easy runs at a conversational pace is an important component of using them for recovery. By doing so, you'll be able to maximize the benefits of easy runs and promote optimal recovery and performance in your cross country running training.

Tip 26: Don't underestimate the importance of easy runs.

In the world of cross country running, it can be easy to get caught up in the intensity and excitement of high-intensity workouts and races. However, it's important not to underestimate the value of easy runs in your training plan.

Easy runs, also known as recovery runs, are an essential component of any cross country runner's training plan. They are lower-intensity runs designed to allow your body to recover from the stress of high-intensity workouts and races. Easy runs help to promote blood flow, reduce muscle soreness and inflammation, and improve your overall aerobic fitness.

One common mistake that many runners make is failing to incorporate enough easy runs into their training plan. It's important to remember that every workout doesn't need to be a high-intensity, high-mileage endeavor. In fact, running too hard or too often can lead to burnout, injury, and a plateau in performance.

Easy runs offer several benefits beyond just recovery. They can help you maintain a healthy body composition by burning fat for energy, improve your mental and emotional well-being, and even boost your confidence by allowing you to enjoy the run and take in your surroundings.

By incorporating easy runs into your training plan and taking them seriously, you'll be able to maximize the benefits of your workouts and races and ultimately achieve your running goals. Remember to keep your easy runs at a conversational pace, listen to your body, and adjust your pace and distance as needed to ensure that you're recovering properly. Don't underestimate the importance of easy runs in your cross country running training plan, and you'll be on your way to becoming a stronger and more successful runner.

Strength Training and Cross-Training

Tip 27: Use heart rate zone training to your advantage

Cross country running is a demanding sport that requires both physical and mental strength. To excel in this sport, runners must employ different training techniques that will help them improve their endurance, speed, and overall performance. One of the most effective methods for training in cross country running is heart rate zone training.

Heart rate zone training involves monitoring your heart rate during exercise and training in specific heart rate zones. This approach allows you to control the intensity of your workouts and optimize your training for maximum results. There are different heart rate zones, ranging from zone 1 (the lowest intensity) to zone 5 (the highest intensity).

To use heart rate zone training to your advantage in cross country running, you need first to determine your maximum heart rate. To do this, subtract your age from 220. Once you know your maximum heart rate, you can determine your target heart rate zones based on your training goals. For example, if you want to improve your endurance, you will need to train in zone 2-3, which is around 60-80% of your maximum heart rate. On the other hand, if you want to improve your speed, you will need to train in zone 4-5, which is around 80-100% of your maximum heart rate.

Using heart rate zone training will help you avoid overtraining, reduce your risk of injury, and improve your overall performance. By training in specific heart rate zones, you will be able to target different aspects of your fitness and gradually improve your endurance, speed, and recovery.

In summary, heart rate zone training is an essential technique that every cross country runner should incorporate into their training regimen. By using this approach, you will be able to optimize your training and achieve your goals more effectively. So, monitor your heart rate, determine your target heart rate zones, and start training like a pro!

Tip 28: Incorporate strength training into your routine.

In addition to running, incorporating strength training into your cross country running routine can have numerous benefits for your performance and overall health. Strength training can help improve your muscular endurance, increase your power and speed, reduce the risk of injury, and even improve your bone density.

When incorporating strength training into your routine, it's important to focus on exercises that target the muscles used while running. These include exercises that strengthen your core, legs, and hips, such as squats, lunges, deadlifts, and planks. In addition, incorporating exercises that target your upper body, such as push-ups and pull-ups, can also be beneficial for maintaining good posture and balance while running.

It's important to start with lighter weights and gradually increase the resistance as your strength improves. Aim to do strength training exercises at least twice a week, allowing for adequate rest and recovery time between sessions.

One common misconception about strength training is that it will make you bulkier and slower as a runner. However, this is not necessarily true. When done correctly, strength training can help you develop lean muscle mass, which can actually improve your running economy and overall performance.

In addition to traditional weight lifting, incorporating bodyweight exercises such as squats, lunges, and planks can be just as effective for improving your strength and endurance. Plyometric exercises such as jump squats and box jumps can also be beneficial for developing explosive power.

Incorporating strength training into your cross country running routine may require some extra time and effort, but the benefits can be well worth it. By improving your muscular strength and endurance, you'll be able to run faster, longer, and with less risk of injury.

Tip 29: Focus on exercises that target your legs and core.

When it comes to strength training for cross country running, it's important to focus on exercises that target your legs and core muscles. These are the muscles that are most used and stressed during running and are essential for maintaining proper form and technique, improving speed, and preventing injuries.

Some effective leg-strengthening exercises include squats, lunges, deadlifts, and calf raises. These exercises help to build strength and endurance in the major muscle groups of the legs, such as the quadriceps, hamstrings, glutes, and calves.

Core-strengthening exercises are also essential for cross country runners. These exercises help to improve your balance, stability, and posture, which are all critical for efficient running form. Some effective core-strengthening exercises include planks, sit-ups, Russian twists, and bicycle crunches.

It's important to start with light weights and proper form, gradually increasing the weight as your strength improves. Bodyweight exercises can also be effective for strength training and can be done anywhere without the need for equipment.

Incorporating leg and core strengthening exercises into your cross country running routine can help to improve your performance and reduce the risk of injuries. However, it's important to remember that strength training should not be done at the expense of your running workouts. It's essential to balance both types of training and allow for adequate rest and recovery time between sessions.

Tip 30: Cross-train to reduce the risk of injury.

Cross-training is an excellent way to reduce the risk of injury in cross country running. It allows you to improve your fitness and build strength while giving your running muscles a break from the repetitive stress of running. Cross-training can also help you recover from injuries and stay in shape when you need to take time off from running.

Some effective cross-training activities for cross country runners include cycling, swimming, rowing, and elliptical training. These low-impact activities can help to maintain and even improve your cardiovascular fitness without putting the same stress on your joints as running. Yoga and Pilates can also be beneficial for improving flexibility, balance, and core strength.

It's important to remember that cross-training should not be used as a substitute for running workouts. While it can be a great addition to your training routine, it's still essential to get in regular running workouts to prepare for races and build specific endurance.

When incorporating cross-training into your cross country running routine, it's important to start slowly and gradually increase the duration and intensity of your cross-training sessions. Aim for at least two to three cross-training sessions per week, but be sure to listen to your body and adjust the frequency and intensity as needed.

In conclusion, cross-training is an effective way to reduce the risk of injury and improve your overall fitness as a cross country runner. By incorporating a variety of low-impact activities into your training routine, you can improve your endurance, build strength, and prevent injuries, all while giving your running muscles the break they need.

Chapter Review

- Building a strong foundation before increasing intensity is essential to prevent injuries and improve performance. Starting with a base mileage and gradually increasing your weekly mileage is a good way to build this foundation.
- Incorporating long runs into your training can help improve your endurance and prepare you for race day. It's important to gradually increase your long run distance and keep your pace at an easy, conversational level.
- Cross-training can be a great addition to your training routine, helping to reduce the risk of injury and improve overall fitness. Activities like cycling, swimming, and yoga can be effective cross-training exercises.
- Strength training, with a focus on exercises that target your legs and core, can help improve your running form and speed and reduce the risk of injury. Starting with light weights and proper form is important to avoid injury.
- Don't underestimate the importance of easy runs for recovery. These runs at a conversational pace are essential for allowing your body to recover and reducing the risk of injury.

Chapter 3: Gear and Nutrition for Cross Country Running

Essential Gear for Cross Country Running

Tip 31: Choose appropriate footwear for the terrain.

One of the most crucial aspects of cross country running is choosing the right footwear. The terrain of the course can have a significant impact on your performance, so it's essential to select appropriate shoes that can handle the challenges of the course.

The type of shoe you need will depend on the terrain of the course. For example, if you're running on a relatively flat and dry surface, you may be able to wear shoes with less tread. However, if you're running on a course with hills, mud, or other obstacles, you'll need shoes with more grip and traction.

When shopping for cross country shoes, it's important to consider the fit and comfort of the shoe. Make sure the shoe fits snugly but not too tight and has enough room in the toe box to prevent blisters. Additionally, look for shoes with adequate cushioning to reduce the impact on your joints and prevent injuries.

Another important factor to consider is the weight of the shoe. Lightweight shoes can help you run faster, but they may not provide enough support for the terrain. On the other hand, heavier shoes can provide more stability and protection but may slow you down.

In addition to the shoe itself, it's important to consider the type of socks you wear. For example, moisture-wicking socks can help keep your feet dry and prevent blisters, while compression socks can improve blood flow and reduce fatigue.

Ultimately, the right shoes can make a significant difference in your performance and comfort during a cross country race. Take the time to find the right pair that fits well, provides adequate support, and is appropriate for the course terrain. With the right shoes, you'll be able to tackle any course with confidence and ease.

Tip 32: Select clothing for various weather conditions.

As a cross country runner, you're at the mercy of the weather. From hot and humid to cold and rainy, the weather can impact your performance and comfort during a race. Therefore, it's crucial to choose the appropriate clothing for different weather conditions.

For hot and humid weather, lightweight and breathable clothing is key. Look for shorts and tops made from moisture-wicking material that can help keep you dry and cool. Avoid cotton, as it tends to trap moisture and can cause chafing. Additionally, consider wearing a hat or visor to protect your face and eyes from the sun.

On the other hand, cold and windy weather requires more insulation and layers. Start with a moisture-wicking base layer, followed by a warm mid-layer like a fleece or jacket. Finally, add a waterproof and windproof outer layer to protect you from the elements. Don't forget to cover your head and hands with a hat and gloves, as they can lose heat quickly.

For rainy weather, a waterproof and breathable jacket is a must-have. Look for one with sealed seams to prevent water from seeping in. Additionally, wear a moisture-wicking base layer and quick-drying shorts or pants. Finally, consider adding a hat with a brim to protect your face from the rain.

In snowy weather, dress in layers to stay warm and dry. Start with a moisture-wicking base layer, followed by an insulating mid-layer, and finish with a waterproof and windproof outer layer. Don't forget to cover your head, hands, and feet with appropriate gear to prevent frostbite.

Lastly, for races held during the transition seasons, such as spring and fall, it's essential to be prepared for sudden weather changes. Bring multiple layers to add or remove as needed. Look for lightweight jackets that can be easily packed away and gloves that can be easily stored in a pocket.

In summary, choosing the appropriate clothing for various weather conditions is crucial for a comfortable and successful cross country race. Consider the temperature, humidity, wind, and precipitation, and choose clothing that is breathable, moisture-wicking, and weather-resistant.

Tip 33: Invest in a quality watch or GPS device.

One of the most important tools for any cross country runner is a watch or GPS device. Whether you're training for a race or running in one, these devices can help you track your progress, measure your pace, and monitor your heart rate.

When choosing a watch or GPS device, it's important to consider your needs and budget. There are many options available, ranging from basic stopwatches to high-tech GPS devices with multiple features. Consider what features are important to you, such as distance tracking, heart rate monitoring, or smartwatch capabilities.

Investing in a quality watch or GPS device can help you track your progress and improve your performance. You can set goals and track your progress over time, helping you to stay motivated and focused on your training. Additionally, these devices can help you monitor your heart rate, helping you to stay within your target heart rate zone and avoid overexertion.

Another benefit of a quality watch or GPS device is that it can help you navigate through unfamiliar routes. Some GPS devices have maps and turn-by-turn directions, helping you to stay on course and avoid getting lost.

When shopping for a watch or GPS device, consider the durability and battery life of the device. You don't want your device to break or run out of battery mid-race or training session. Additionally, make sure the device is comfortable to wear and easy to use, as you'll be wearing it for long periods of time.

In summary, investing in a quality watch or GPS device can help you improve your performance and achieve your goals in cross country running. Consider your needs and budget when choosing a device, and look for features like distance tracking, heart rate monitoring, and navigational capabilities. With the right device, you'll be able to track your progress, stay motivated, and achieve your best results.

Tip 34: Consider hydration options, such as handheld water bottles or hydration packs.

Proper hydration is critical for any cross country runner. It's essential to stay hydrated during training and races to maintain performance and prevent dehydration. Therefore, it's important to consider hydration options, such as handheld water bottles or hydration packs.

Handheld water bottles are a popular choice for runners who prefer a minimalist approach. They are easy to carry and allow for quick access to water during a run. Handheld bottles come in different sizes and designs, so it's important to choose one that is comfortable and fits your needs.

Hydration packs are another option for runners who need more water or prefer to carry their gear on their backs. These packs come in different sizes and designs and can hold water, snacks, and other essentials. Hydration packs are a good choice for long runs or races where water stations may be scarce.

When choosing a hydration option, it's important to consider factors such as comfort, convenience, and capacity. Look for a hydration solution that is easy to use and comfortable to wear.

Additionally, make sure it's the right size to hold enough water for your needs without being too heavy or bulky.

It's also important to remember to hydrate before, during, and after your run. Drink plenty of water before your run to ensure you're starting off hydrated. During your run, aim to drink water every 20-30 minutes or as needed. After your run, replenish fluids with water or a sports drink to help restore electrolytes.

In summary, considering hydration options is important for any cross country runner. Handheld water bottles and hydration packs are popular choices that offer convenience and comfort. Make sure to choose a hydration solution that fits your needs, and remember to hydrate before, during, and after your run to maintain performance and prevent dehydration.

Proper Nutrition for Cross Country Running

Tip 35: Carbohydrates: The importance of carbs for energy.

Carbohydrates are a crucial source of energy for cross country runners. Carbohydrates are converted into glucose, which is the primary fuel source for muscles during exercise. Therefore, consuming enough carbohydrates is essential for maintaining energy levels and endurance during training and races.

It's recommended that carbohydrates should make up around 45-65% of a runner's daily caloric intake. This means that if you're a runner who consumes 2,000 calories per day, you should aim to consume between 900-1,300 calories from carbohydrates.

Carbohydrates can be found in a variety of foods, including bread, pasta, rice, fruits, and vegetables. Complex carbohydrates, such as whole-grain bread and pasta, provide a slower release of energy compared to simple carbohydrates, such as sugar and candy.

It's important to consume carbohydrates before, during, and after your run. Eating a carbohydrate-rich meal 2-3 hours before your run can help top off your glycogen stores and provide sustained energy throughout your run. During your run, consuming carbohydrates like sports drinks or energy gels can help maintain energy levels and delay fatigue. After your run, consuming carbohydrates can help replenish glycogen stores and aid in muscle recovery.

It's also important to note that not all carbohydrates are created equal. Choosing nutrient-dense, whole-food sources of carbohydrates is essential for optimal health and performance. Additionally, consuming too many simple carbohydrates, such as sugary drinks and candy, can lead to a rapid increase in blood sugar levels, followed by a crash in energy levels.

In summary, carbohydrates are an important source of energy for cross country runners. Consuming enough carbohydrates through whole-food sources can help maintain energy levels and endurance during training and races. Remember to consume carbohydrates before, during, and after your run, and choose nutrient-dense sources for optimal health and performance.

Tip 36: Protein: The role of protein in muscle repair and recovery.

Protein is an essential macronutrient that plays a critical role in muscle repair and recovery for cross country runners. During exercise, the muscle fibers in your body undergo damage and breakdown, and protein is necessary for repairing and rebuilding these fibers.

Protein is made up of amino acids, the building blocks of muscles. Consuming enough protein is crucial for the repair and growth of muscle tissue. Protein also plays a role in the synthesis of enzymes, hormones, and other essential molecules in the body.

As a cross country runner, it's important to consume enough protein to support muscle repair and recovery. The amount of protein needed varies depending on factors such as body weight, activity level, and training goals. A general guideline is to consume 1.2-1.7 grams of protein per kilogram of body weight per day.

Protein can be found in a variety of foods, including meat, poultry, fish, eggs, dairy products, legumes, and nuts. It's important to choose lean sources of protein, such as skinless chicken, fish, and legumes, to avoid excess fat intake.

The timing of protein intake is also important for muscle repair and recovery. Consuming protein shortly after exercise can help jumpstart the recovery process. For example, research has shown that consuming protein within 30 minutes of exercise can improve muscle protein synthesis and promote recovery.

In summary, protein plays a critical role in muscle repair and recovery for cross country runners. Consuming enough protein through lean sources such as meat, poultry, fish, eggs, dairy products, legumes, and nuts is important for maintaining muscle mass and promoting recovery. Timing of protein intake is also crucial, with consuming protein shortly after exercise being optimal for muscle repair and recovery.

Tip 37: Healthy fats: How fats can provide long-lasting energy.

While carbohydrates are the primary source of energy for cross country runners, healthy fats can also provide long-lasting energy and play a crucial role in overall health.

Healthy fats, such as monounsaturated and polyunsaturated fats, are beneficial for runners because they provide a sustained source of energy. Unlike simple carbohydrates, which can provide a quick energy boost but are quickly metabolized, fats are metabolized more slowly, providing a steady source of energy over a longer period of time.

Additionally, healthy fats are important for overall health and well-being. They are essential for the absorption of fat-soluble vitamins, such as vitamins A, D, E, and K. They also play a role in the production of hormones and the maintenance of healthy cell membranes.

Healthy sources of fats include nuts and seeds, avocados, olive oil, fatty fish, and coconut oil. It's important to choose whole food sources of fats rather than processed or fried foods, which can be high in unhealthy fats and contribute to inflammation and other health issues.

While healthy fats are important for cross country runners, it's still important to consume them in moderation. Fats are more calorie-dense than carbohydrates or protein, so consuming too much fat can lead to weight gain and decreased performance.

In summary, healthy fats can provide a sustained source of energy for cross country runners and are important for overall health and well-being. Choosing whole food sources of fats, such as nuts and seeds, avocados, and fatty fish, is important for optimal health and performance. However, it's still important to consume fats in moderation to avoid excess calorie intake.

Tip 38: Hydration: The importance of staying hydrated during runs.

Staying hydrated during runs is crucial for cross country runners to maintain optimal performance and prevent dehydration-related health issues. When you run, your body loses water through sweat, and if you don't replace that lost fluid, it can lead to dehydration, which can cause fatigue, cramping, and even heat exhaustion or heat stroke.

It's important to drink water before, during, and after your run to avoid dehydration. The amount of water needed depends on factors such as body weight, activity level, and temperature. Still, a general guideline is to aim for at least 16-20 ounces of water 2-3 hours before your run and then 6-8 ounces of water every 20-30 minutes during your run.

In addition to water, electrolytes are also important for maintaining hydration and optimal performance. Electrolytes, such as sodium, potassium, and magnesium, help regulate fluid balance in the body and are lost through sweat. Consuming electrolyte-rich fluids, such as sports drinks or coconut water, can help replenish these lost electrolytes and maintain hydration.

Signs of dehydration include dark urine, dry mouth and throat, headache, dizziness, and fatigue. If you experience any of these symptoms during your run, it's important to stop and rehydrate immediately.

In summary, staying hydrated during runs is crucial for cross country runners to maintain optimal performance and prevent dehydration-related health issues. Drinking water before, during, and after your run, as well as consuming electrolyte-rich fluids, can help maintain hydration and replace lost fluids and electrolytes. Be aware of the signs of dehydration and take action immediately if you experience any symptoms.

Tip 39: Timing: The best times to eat before and after runs.

Timing your meals before and after runs is important for cross country runners to optimize performance and recovery.

Before your run, it's best to eat a meal high in carbohydrates, moderate in protein, and low in fat. This will provide your body with the energy it needs to power through your run without causing digestive issues. In addition, it's recommended to eat a meal 2-3 hours before your run to allow time for digestion. Some examples of pre-run meals include oatmeal with fruit, a smoothie with banana and yogurt, or a turkey sandwich on whole-grain bread.

If you don't have time for a full meal before your run, a small snack 30 minutes to an hour before your run can still provide your body with the energy it needs. Some examples of pre-run snacks include a banana, a granola bar, or a handful of pretzels.

After your run, it's important to refuel your body with a meal high in carbohydrates and protein to help repair and rebuild muscle tissue. It's recommended to eat a meal within 30 minutes to an hour after your run to optimize recovery. Some examples of post-run meals include a chicken quinoa bowl with vegetables, a tuna sandwich on whole grain bread, or a sweet potato with black beans and avocado.

In addition to meals, hydration is also important before and after runs. Be sure to drink water before your run and consume fluids and electrolytes after your run to replace lost fluids.

In summary, timing your meals before and after runs is important for cross country runners to optimize performance and recovery. Eating a meal high in carbohydrates, moderate in protein, and low in fat 2-3 hours before your run can provide your body with the energy it needs.

Consuming a post-run meal high in carbohydrates and protein within 30 minutes to an hour after your run can help repair and rebuild muscle tissue. Don't forget to hydrate before and after your run as well.

Pre- and Post-Run Nutrition

Tip 40: Pre-run meals: The importance of fueling up before a run.

Fueling up with a pre-run meal is crucial for cross country runners to optimize their energy levels and performance during their run. Eating the right foods before a run can help provide your body with the necessary carbohydrates and nutrients to sustain you throughout your run.

The ideal pre-run meal should consist of easily digestible carbohydrates and a moderate amount of protein and be low in fat and fiber. Carbohydrates are essential for providing your body with energy and should make up the majority of your pre-run meal. Protein helps to repair and build muscle tissue and can also help to slow down the absorption of carbohydrates, providing you with sustained energy throughout your run.

It is recommended to eat your pre-run meal 2-3 hours before your run to allow for proper digestion. Some examples of pre-run meals include a bagel with peanut butter, banana and honey, oatmeal with fruit and nuts, or a smoothie made with fruit, yogurt, and protein powder.

If you don't have enough time to eat a full meal before your run, you can still provide your body with the necessary fuel by eating a small snack 30 minutes to an hour before your run. Some examples of pre-run snacks include a banana, an energy bar, or a small bowl of cereal with milk.

Skipping a pre-run meal can cause your energy levels to dip and lead to fatigue, which can negatively impact your performance. It can also cause stomach discomfort or digestive issues during your run.

In summary, fueling up with a pre-run meal is crucial for cross country runners to optimize their energy levels and performance. Eating the right foods, such as easily digestible carbohydrates and a moderate amount of protein, 2-3 hours before your run can provide you with sustained energy. Don't skip your pre-run meal, as it can negatively impact your performance and cause digestive issues.

Tip 41: Post-run meals: The importance of refueling and repairing your body after a run.

Refueling and repairing your body after a run is just as important as fueling up before your run. The post-run meal should consist of carbohydrates to replenish depleted glycogen stores and protein to help repair and rebuild muscle tissue. Consuming a post-run meal within 30 minutes to an hour after your run can optimize recovery and reduce muscle soreness.

Carbohydrates are essential for replenishing depleted glycogen stores, which are the primary fuel source for muscles during exercise. Aim to consume 0.5-0.75 grams of carbohydrates per pound of body weight post-run. Some examples of carbohydrate-rich foods include whole-grain bread, pasta, rice, fruits, and vegetables.

Protein is essential for repairing and rebuilding muscle tissue that may have been damaged during exercise. Aim to consume 15-25 grams of protein post-run. Some examples of protein-rich foods include chicken, fish, eggs, beans, and tofu.

In addition to carbohydrates and protein, healthy fats and fluids are also important for recovery. Healthy fats, such as those found in nuts, seeds, and avocados, can provide long-lasting energy and aid in nutrient absorption. Hydrating with water or a sports drink can help replace fluids and electrolytes lost during exercise.

Some examples of post-run meals include a turkey sandwich on whole grain bread with avocado and vegetables, grilled salmon with quinoa and roasted vegetables, or a smoothie made with banana, yogurt, and protein powder.

Skipping a post-run meal can delay recovery and increase the risk of injury. It can also cause increased muscle soreness and fatigue during subsequent workouts.

In summary, refueling and repairing your body after a run is just as important as fueling up before your run. Consuming a post-run meal with carbohydrates and protein within 30 minutes to an hour after your run can optimize recovery and reduce muscle soreness. Don't skip your post-run meal, and aim to include healthy fats and fluids as well.

Tip 42: Snacks for on-the-go: Quick and easy snacks for during and runs.

Having quick and easy snacks on hand during and after runs can help provide a quick energy boost and aid in recovery. Here are some examples of snacks for on-the-go:

1. Energy bars or gels: Energy bars and gels are a convenient and quick source of carbohydrates and can be easily carried in a pocket or running belt. Look for bars or gels that contain a mix of carbohydrates, protein, and healthy fats.
2. Trail mix: Trail mix is a great option for a quick snack that combines carbohydrates, protein, and healthy fats. Make your own mix with nuts, seeds, dried fruit, and a few chocolate chips for a sweet treat.
3. Bananas: Bananas are a great source of carbohydrates and can provide a quick energy boost. They also contain potassium, which can help replace electrolytes lost during exercise.
4. Greek yogurt: Greek yogurt is high in protein and can help aid in muscle recovery. Look for individual cups or pack a small container with your favorite toppings, such as fruit and granola.
5. Peanut butter and crackers: Peanut butter is a good source of protein and healthy fats, and crackers can provide carbohydrates. Pack a small container of peanut butter and a few crackers for a quick and easy snack.
6. Fruit: Fresh fruit, such as apples or oranges, can provide carbohydrates and hydration. They are also a good source of vitamins and minerals.
7. Chocolate milk: Chocolate milk is a great post-run recovery drink, providing a mix of carbohydrates, protein, and fluids. Pack a small carton or bottle for a quick and easy post-run snack.

In summary, having quick and easy snacks on hand during and after runs can help provide a quick energy boost and aid in recovery. Energy bars or gels, trail mix, bananas, Greek yogurt, peanut butter and crackers, fresh fruit, and chocolate milk are all great options for on-the-go snacking.

Tip 43: Supplements: How supplements can complement your nutrition plan.

While it's important to focus on getting nutrients from whole foods, supplements can be a useful addition to a nutrition plan for runners. Supplements can help fill any nutritional gaps and complement your nutrition plan. Here are some supplements that can benefit runners:

1. Multivitamin: A high-quality multivitamin can help fill any gaps in your nutrition plan and ensure you're getting all the necessary vitamins and minerals for optimal health and performance.
2. Omega-3 fatty acids: Omega-3 fatty acids can help reduce inflammation and improve cardiovascular health. They can be found in fatty fish, such as salmon and tuna, but supplements can be a useful addition for those who don't consume enough fish in their diet.
3. Vitamin D: Vitamin D is important for bone health and immune function. It can be found in sunlight and certain foods, but supplements can be helpful for those who don't get enough exposure to sunlight or consume enough vitamin D-rich foods.
4. Creatine: Creatine can help improve performance in high-intensity activities, such as sprinting or weightlifting. It can also help with muscle recovery and growth. Creatine is naturally found in red meat and fish, but supplements can be a convenient way to ensure you're getting enough.
5. Protein powder: Protein powder can be a convenient way to supplement your diet with additional protein. It can help aid in muscle recovery and growth and can be useful for those who have difficulty meeting their daily protein needs through food alone.

It's important to note that supplements should not replace a healthy, balanced diet. Always talk to your doctor or a registered dietitian before starting any new supplement regimen. They can help determine if supplements are necessary and recommend safe and effective dosages.

In summary, supplements can be a useful addition to a nutrition plan for runners. Multivitamins, omega-3 fatty acids, vitamin D, creatine, and protein powder are examples of supplements that can complement a healthy diet and improve performance and recovery. However, it's important to talk to a healthcare professional before starting any new supplement regimen.

Chapter Review

- Nutrition is an essential part of a runner's training plan and can help improve performance and aid in recovery.
- Carbohydrates are the main source of energy for runners and should make up the majority of their diet.
- Protein is crucial for muscle repair and recovery and should be included in every meal and snack.
- Healthy fats can provide long-lasting energy and aid in recovery but should be consumed in moderation.
- Supplements can complement a healthy diet and help fill any nutritional gaps, but they should not replace whole foods. Always consult with a healthcare professional before starting a new supplement regimen.

Chapter 4: Improving Your Speed and Technique

Interval Training

Tip 44: Start with a warm-up: Always begin with a proper warm-up to prevent injury and prepare your body for the workout ahead.

Cross country running is a challenging and physically demanding sport that requires a lot of dedication, discipline, and endurance. It involves running on natural terrains, such as hills, trails, and fields, which makes it a unique and exciting experience for athletes of all levels. Whether you are a beginner or an experienced runner, one of the most important tips to keep in mind is to always start with a proper warm-up.

Before starting your workout, it is essential to prepare your body by raising your heart rate, increasing blood flow to your muscles, and loosening up your joints. This can be achieved through a dynamic warm-up routine that includes activities such as jogging, jumping jacks, lunges, and stretching. A proper warm-up will not only help you prevent injuries but will also improve your performance during the workout ahead.

It is important to note that a warm-up should not be rushed or skipped altogether. Taking the time to prepare your body for the physical demands of cross country running will make a significant difference in your overall experience. Additionally, a warm-up routine can be tailored to fit your specific needs and goals. For example, if you are preparing for a race or competition, you may want to include drills that focus on speed and agility.

In summary, starting with a proper warm-up is a crucial tip for anyone interested in cross country running. It will help you prevent injuries, improve your performance, and make your overall experience more enjoyable. Remember to take the time to prepare your body before every workout and tailor your warm-up routine to fit your specific needs and goals. With this tip in mind, you are one step closer to becoming a successful cross country runner.

Tip 45: Choose the right distance: When it comes to interval training, the distance you choose should be based on your fitness level and goals.

Interval training is a popular method of improving cardiovascular fitness and endurance in cross country running. It involves alternating between periods of high-intensity exercise and rest or low-intensity exercise. One of the keys to effective interval training is choosing the right distance for your intervals. This tip emphasizes the importance of tailoring your interval distances to your fitness level and goals.

If you are new to interval training or have a lower fitness level, starting with shorter distances is recommended. For example, 200-meter sprints or 400-meter runs followed by a period of rest or low-intensity exercise could be a good starting point. Then, as your fitness level improves, you can gradually increase the distance of your intervals. This will challenge your body and help you reach your goals faster.

On the other hand, if you are an experienced runner or have a specific goal in mind, such as preparing for a race or competition, you may want to focus on longer intervals. For example, 800-meter or 1,000-meter runs followed by a period of rest or low-intensity exercise could be appropriate. These longer intervals will help you build endurance and prepare you for the demands of a longer race.

It's essential to note that the distance of your intervals should also align with your goals. If your goal is to improve your speed, shorter intervals with higher intensity may be more effective. If your goal is to improve your endurance, longer intervals with lower intensity may be more beneficial.

In summary, choosing the right distance for your intervals is a critical tip for effective interval training in cross country running. Tailoring the distance of your intervals to your fitness level and goals will help you achieve optimal results. Remember to start with shorter intervals if you are new to interval training and gradually increase the distance as your fitness level improves. Always keep your goals in mind when choosing your interval distances, and enjoy the benefits of a successful interval training program.

Tip 46: Incorporate recovery periods: Allow yourself ample time to recover between intervals to prevent fatigue and injury.

In cross country running, interval training is an effective way to improve endurance, speed, and overall performance. However, it's important to remember that the recovery period between intervals is just as crucial as the high-intensity intervals themselves. This tip emphasizes the importance of incorporating recovery periods into your interval training routine to prevent fatigue and injury.

During high-intensity intervals, your body undergoes significant stress, leading to the production of lactic acid and a depletion of energy stores. Recovery periods allow your body to remove this lactic acid and replenish energy stores, which is essential for avoiding fatigue and injury. Therefore, it's important to allow yourself ample time to recover between intervals.

The duration of recovery periods between intervals can vary based on your fitness level and goals. If you're new to interval training, starting with longer recovery periods (i.e., 2-3 minutes) may be more appropriate. As you become more experienced, you can gradually decrease the duration of your recovery periods (i.e., 1-2 minutes) to increase the intensity of your workout.

It's also important to use active recovery during your rest periods. Rather than coming to a complete stop, light jogging or walking can help you maintain blood flow and improve recovery time.

Additionally, stretching and hydration are essential during rest periods to prevent muscle soreness and dehydration.

In summary, incorporating recovery periods into your interval training routine is a critical tip for preventing fatigue and injury. Adequate recovery periods allow your body to remove lactic acid, replenish energy stores, and prevent overexertion. Remember to tailor your recovery periods to your fitness level and goals, use active recovery techniques, and incorporate stretching and hydration to maintain optimal performance. With these tips in mind, you'll be able to create a successful interval training program in cross country running.

Tip 47: Gradually increase your speed: As you become more comfortable with interval training, gradually increase your speed to challenge yourself and improve your overall speed.

Interval training is a powerful tool for improving speed and endurance in cross country running. As you become more comfortable with this type of training, it's important to gradually increase your speed to keep challenging yourself and achieve your performance goals. This tip emphasizes the importance of gradually increasing your speed during interval training to improve overall speed and performance.

When you first start interval training, it's important to focus on developing proper form and technique while maintaining a comfortable pace. Once you've established a solid foundation, you can begin to increase your speed during high-intensity intervals gradually. This can be done by increasing your pace by a small increment each session or by setting a goal pace for each interval and working towards that pace over time.

It's important to note that increasing speed too quickly can lead to injury and burnout. Gradual and incremental increases in speed are much safer and more effective for long-term improvements. Additionally, it's important to balance speed work with recovery periods and low-intensity exercise to prevent overexertion and maintain a consistent training routine.

Another effective way to gradually increase your speed is by incorporating different types of interval workouts, such as tempo runs or fartlek. These workouts allow you to vary your pace and challenge yourself in different ways, which can help break through speed plateaus and improve overall performance.

In summary, gradually increasing your speed during interval training is a key tip for improving overall speed and performance in cross country running. Remember to focus on proper form and technique before increasing speed, increase speed gradually and incrementally, balance speed work with recovery periods, and consider incorporating different types of interval workouts to challenge yourself in different ways. With these tips in mind, you'll be on your way to achieving your cross country running goals.

Tip 48: Keep track of your progress: Keep a record of your workouts to track your progress and see how far you've come.

Keeping track of your progress is an important aspect of any training program, including cross country running. By tracking your workouts, you can monitor your progress, identify areas of improvement, and celebrate your achievements. This tip emphasizes the importance of keeping a record of your workouts to help you track your progress and stay motivated.

There are many different ways to keep track of your workouts, such as using a training log, a smartphone app, or an online tool. Whatever method you choose, make sure to record important information such as the distance, time, pace, and any other relevant notes about your workout.

By keeping track of your workouts, you can monitor your progress over time. For example, you might notice that you're running faster or longer distances than before or that you're recovering more quickly between intervals. Seeing this progress can be incredibly motivating and help you stay committed to your training routine.

Tracking your workouts can also help you identify areas of improvement. For example, you might notice that you struggle with hill workouts or maintaining a consistent pace. With this knowledge, you can adjust your training program to focus on those areas and work towards improving them.

Finally, keeping a record of your workouts allows you to celebrate your achievements. Cross country running is a challenging sport, and every milestone deserves recognition. Whether it's completing your first 5K or setting a new personal best, taking the time to acknowledge your progress can help keep you motivated and committed to your training.

In summary, keeping track of your workouts is an important tip for cross country runners who want to monitor their progress and stay motivated. Remember to record important information about each workout, monitor your progress over time, identify areas of improvement, and celebrate your achievements. With these tips in mind, you'll be able to stay focused, motivated, and committed to achieving your cross country running goals.

Tempo Runs

Tip 49: Find the right tempo: The pace of your tempo runs should be challenging but still sustainable for a longer period of time.

Tempo runs are a key component of any cross country training program, and finding the right tempo pace is crucial for improving speed, endurance, and overall performance. This tip emphasizes the importance of finding the right tempo pace that is challenging but still sustainable for a longer period of time.

A tempo run is a sustained effort at a moderately high intensity, typically lasting between 20 and 60 minutes. The goal of a tempo run is to improve your lactate threshold, which is the point at which your body starts to produce more lactate than it can clear, leading to fatigue and decreased performance. By running at a sustained, challenging pace, you can raise your lactate threshold, allowing you to run faster for longer periods of time.

When finding your tempo pace, it's important to choose a pace that is challenging but still sustainable for a longer period of time. This pace should be faster than your usual easy or recovery pace but not so fast that you're unable to maintain it for the duration of the run. A good rule of thumb is to aim for a pace that feels comfortably hard, where you're breathing deeply but still able to speak in short sentences.

To determine your tempo pace, you can use a variety of methods such as heart rate monitoring, perceived exertion, or pace charts. It's important to experiment with different methods and find the one that works best for you. Additionally, as your fitness level improves, you may need to adjust your tempo pace to continue challenging yourself.

In summary, finding the right tempo pace is a key tip for improving speed, endurance, and overall performance in cross country running. Remember to choose a pace that is challenging but still sustainable for a longer period of time, experiment with different methods for determining your pace, and adjust your tempo pace as your fitness level improves. With these tips in mind, you'll be able to incorporate effective tempo runs into your cross country training program and see improvements in your performance.

Tip 50: Incorporate a warm-up and cool-down: Like all workouts, it's important to warm up and cool down before and after your tempo runs.

Warming up and cooling down before and after your tempo runs is an important tip for cross country runners who want to prevent injury, improve performance, and aid in recovery. A proper warm-up and cool-down can help prepare your body for the workout ahead and help it recover more quickly afterward.

When warming up before your tempo run, you should start with some light aerobic exercise to get your heart rate, and muscles warmed up. This could include a few minutes of jogging, jumping jacks, or dynamic stretching exercises that mimic the movements you'll be doing during your workout. Then, gradually increase the intensity of your warm-up, but avoid doing anything too strenuous that could tire you out before your tempo run.

After your tempo run, it's important to cool down to help your body recover and prevent injury. You can do this by gradually reducing the intensity of your workout, followed by some light aerobic exercises and static stretching exercises that help to stretch out your muscles. This can help prevent stiffness and soreness and reduce your risk of injury.

By incorporating a warm-up and cool-down into your tempo runs, you can help your body prepare for the workout ahead and recover more quickly afterward. A proper warm-up and cool-down can also help improve your performance by increasing blood flow to your muscles, improving your range of motion, and reducing your risk of injury.

In summary, incorporating a warm-up and cool-down before and after your tempo runs is an important tip for cross country runners. Remember to start with some light aerobic exercise to warm up your body, gradually increase the intensity of your warm-up, and cool down afterward with light aerobic exercise and static stretching. By following these tips, you'll be able to prevent injury, improve performance, and aid in recovery during your tempo runs.

Tip 51: Mix up your workouts: To keep your workouts interesting and challenging, try different types of tempo runs, such as steady state, ladder, and wave tempo runs.

Mixing up your workouts is a great way to keep things interesting and challenge your body in new ways. This tip suggests trying different types of tempo runs, such as steady state, ladder, and wave tempo runs, to add variety to your training and improve your overall performance.

Steady-state tempo runs involve running at a steady pace for a set distance or time, typically between 20 and 60 minutes. This type of tempo run is great for improving your lactate threshold and increasing your overall endurance. You should aim to maintain a consistent pace throughout the run, with only minor variations in speed.

Ladder tempo runs involve gradually increasing and then decreasing your pace over the course of the run. For example, you might start with a five-minute warm-up, then run for three minutes at a moderate pace, followed by two minutes at a faster pace, and then one minute at your fastest pace. You would then repeat the cycle in reverse order until you finish with a five-minute cool-down. This type of tempo run is great for improving your speed, endurance, and mental toughness.

Wave tempo runs involve alternating between periods of faster and slower running. For example, you might start with a five-minute warm-up, then run for one minute at a hard pace, followed by two minutes at an easy pace. You would then repeat this cycle, gradually increasing the length of the hard and easy segments until you reach a peak and then gradually decrease again. This type of tempo run is great for improving your speed and endurance and also adds a fun and challenging element to your training.

By mixing up your workouts with different types of tempo runs, you can challenge your body in new ways and prevent boredom and burnout. Remember to adjust your pace and distance based on your fitness level and goals, and always listen to your body to prevent injury.

In summary, trying different types of tempo runs is a great tip for cross country runners who want to add variety to their training and improve their overall performance. Consider incorporating steady state, ladder, and wave tempo runs into your routine, and always adjust your pace and distance based on your fitness level and goals. With these tips in mind, you'll be able to keep your workouts interesting and challenging and see improvements in your performance.

Tip 52: Focus on form: Pay attention to your form during tempo runs to prevent injury and maximize your speed.

Focusing on form during your tempo runs is an essential tip for any cross country runner who wants to prevent injury and maximize their speed. Proper running form helps to ensure that your body is aligned correctly and that you are using your energy efficiently.

The first aspect of good form is your posture. Keep your head up, your shoulders relaxed, and your chest forward. Avoid slouching or leaning too far forward or backward, as this can strain your back and lead to discomfort.

The next aspect of good form is your foot strike. Aim to land on the midfoot or forefoot rather than the heel, as this will help to reduce the impact on your joints and minimize your risk of injury. Keep your stride short and quick, with your feet landing directly under your body.

Another important element of good form is your arm swing. Your arms should be relaxed and swinging naturally, with your elbows bent at a 90-degree angle. Keep your hands unclenched and avoid crossing them over your body, as this can throw off your balance and waste energy.

Finally, remember to breathe deeply and rhythmically during your tempo runs. Inhale deeply through your nose and exhale forcefully through your mouth, keeping your breathing steady and controlled.

By focusing on your form during your tempo runs, you'll be able to run more efficiently and effectively, reducing your risk of injury and improving your speed. Take the time to pay attention to your posture, foot strike, arm swing, and breathing, and make adjustments as needed. With practice, you'll be able to develop a good form that will carry over into all of your cross country runs.

Tip 53: Use a metronome: A metronome can help you maintain a consistent tempo and prevent you from starting too fast or slowing down too much.

Using a metronome during your tempo runs is a great way to help you maintain a consistent pace and prevent you from starting too fast or slowing down too much. A metronome is a device that produces a steady, rhythmic sound or beep at a set tempo, which can be adjusted to match your desired pace.

To use a metronome, simply set the tempo to match your desired pace and then listen to the rhythmic sound as you run. The sound will help you to stay on pace, and you can adjust your stride accordingly to keep up with the beat.

Using a metronome can be especially helpful for newer runners who may struggle with pacing themselves. It can also be beneficial for more experienced runners who want to improve their pacing skills and avoid starting too fast or slowing down too much during their tempo runs.

In addition to using a metronome during your tempo runs, you can also use it during your warm-up and cool-down to help you establish a consistent cadence and prepare your body for the workout ahead. Just be sure to choose a metronome that is easy to use and adjust and that produces a clear, audible sound that you can hear over your running.

By incorporating a metronome into your tempo runs, you'll be able to maintain a consistent pace, improve your pacing skills, and get the most out of your cross country training. Give it a try and see how it can help you achieve your running goals!

Hill Repeats

Tip 54: Choose the right hill: When selecting a hill for your workout, look for a hill that is challenging but not too steep or too long.

Choosing the right hill for your cross country workout is essential for ensuring you get the most out of your training and avoid injury. When selecting a hill for your workout, it's important to find a hill that is challenging but not too steep or too long.

Ideally, you want to choose a hill that is steep enough to provide a good challenge but not so steep that it puts too much strain on your legs or causes you to lose your form. A hill that is too steep can also increase your risk of injury, particularly if you're not used to running hills.

Similarly, you want to find a hill that is long enough to provide a good workout but not so long that you exhaust yourself before you reach the top. A hill that is too long can also be demotivating, particularly if you're struggling to maintain your pace.

When choosing a hill, consider the length, incline, and terrain. Look for a hill around 200-400 meters long, with an incline of around 4-6%. This will provide a good challenge without being too overwhelming. You may also want to choose a hill with a grassy or dirt surface, as this can provide better traction and reduce your risk of slipping or falling.

Remember to warm up properly before running hills, and start with a few repetitions before gradually increasing the number of repeats as your fitness level improves. And always listen to your body - if a hill feels too challenging or you experience pain or discomfort, slow down or stop and take a break.

By choosing the right hill for your workout, you'll be able to get the most out of your cross country training and improve your strength and endurance.

Tip 55: Use proper form: Focus on using proper form when running uphill, including using your arms and leaning forward slightly.

When running uphill, it's important to use proper form to maximize your efficiency and minimize your risk of injury. Here are some tips on how to maintain proper form when running uphill:

1. Use your arms: Your arms play a crucial role in running uphill. Swing them back and forth in a natural motion, keeping them close to your body. Use them to help drive you up the hill and maintain your balance.
2. Lean forward slightly: Lean forward slightly from the ankles, not the waist, to help you maintain momentum and prevent you from losing your balance.
3. Shorten your stride: When running uphill, it's important to shorten your stride to maintain your cadence and prevent your legs from getting tired too quickly.
4. Keep your head up: Look straight ahead and keep your head up to maintain good posture and prevent your neck from getting tired.
5. Engage your core: Engage your core muscles to help stabilize your body and maintain proper form.

By using these tips, you can maintain proper form when running uphill and make the most of your cross country training. Remember to start with a gradual incline and increase the intensity over time as your fitness level improves. And always listen to your body - if you feel any pain or discomfort, slow down or take a break to avoid injury.

Tip 56: Take breaks when necessary: Don't be afraid to take breaks between hill repeats if you need to catch your breath or rest your legs.

Taking breaks during your cross country hill repeats is a good strategy for preventing injury and allowing your body to recover. It's important to listen to your body and take breaks as necessary rather than pushing yourself too hard and risking injury or burnout.

If you find yourself getting winded or feeling fatigued during a hill repeat, it's perfectly fine to take a break and catch your breath. You can either stop completely or slow down to a walk or jog until you feel ready to continue. This can also be a good opportunity to stretch your legs and prevent muscle soreness.

It's important to remember that taking breaks doesn't mean you're not working hard enough. Cross country hill repeats are a challenging workout, and it's normal to need rest periods in between. By taking breaks when you need them, you'll be able to maintain your form and prevent injuries while still getting a great workout.

When taking breaks, try to keep them brief - a minute or two is usually sufficient. This will help you maintain your momentum and prevent your muscles from cooling down too much. Remember to stay hydrated and listen to your body - if you feel like you need more rest, take it.

By taking breaks as needed during your cross country hill repeats, you'll be able to maintain your fitness and endurance while also staying safe and injury-free.

Tip 57: Gradually increase the number of repeats: Start with a manageable number of hill repeats and gradually increase the number over time.

Gradually increasing the number of hill repeats in your cross country training can help you build endurance and improve your overall fitness. However, it's important to start with a manageable number of repeats and gradually increase the intensity over time.

When beginning hill repeats, start with a number that feels challenging but still manageable. This will help you avoid overexertion and prevent injury. Then, as you become more comfortable with the workout, gradually increase the number of repeats. This could mean adding one or two more repeats per week or per workout, depending on your fitness level.

It's also important to pay attention to how your body is feeling as you increase the number of hill repeats. If you start to feel fatigued or experience any pain or discomfort, it may be a sign that you need to scale back or take a break. Remember to listen to your body and adjust your training accordingly.

In addition to increasing the number of repeats, you can also vary the intensity of your hill workouts. For example, you could increase the incline of the hill, decrease your rest periods, or add additional exercises such as lunges or squats. This will help prevent boredom and challenge your body in new ways.

Remember, gradual progression is key when it comes to hill repeats in cross country running. By starting with a manageable number of repeats and gradually increasing over time, you'll be able to build endurance and improve your overall fitness while also minimizing the risk of injury or burnout.

Tip 58: Celebrate your progress: As you improve your speed and technique through hill repeats, take time to celebrate your progress and give yourself credit for your hard work.

Celebrating your progress is an important part of any training program, including hill repeats in cross country running. When you take the time to acknowledge your progress and celebrate your successes, you can build motivation and confidence, which can help you stay committed to your training goals.

There are many ways to celebrate your progress during hill repeats. You could set small goals for yourself, such as increasing the number of repeats or decreasing your rest time between repeats, and then celebrate when you achieve those goals. You could also reward yourself with something you enjoy, such as a favorite snack or activity, after a particularly challenging hill workout.

In addition to celebrating your progress, it's also important to recognize that progress is not always linear. There will be days when your performance is better than others and times when you may need to adjust your training due to injury, illness, or other factors. It's important to be kind to yourself and focus on the overall progress you've made rather than getting discouraged by setbacks or temporary plateaus.

Remember, cross country running is a challenging sport that requires dedication and hard work. By celebrating your progress during hill repeats and throughout your training, you can build confidence and motivation, which can help you achieve your goals and become a stronger, more confident runner.

Chapter Review

- Choose the right hill: Select a hill that is challenging but not too steep or too long for your hill-repeats workout.

- Focus on proper form: Use proper form when running uphill, including using your arms and leaning forward slightly to maximize your speed and prevent injury.
- Gradually increase the number of repeats: Start with a manageable number of hill repeats and gradually increase the number over time to improve your endurance and speed.
- Take breaks when necessary: Don't be afraid to take breaks between hill repeats if you need to catch your breath or rest your legs.
- Celebrate your progress: Acknowledge your progress during hill repeats and celebrate your successes to build motivation and confidence, which can help you stay committed to your training goals.

Chapter 5: Racing Strategies and Tactics

Pre-Race Nutrition

Tip 59: Hydrate properly: Start hydrating well before your race and continue to drink water leading up to the start.

One of the most critical aspects of running a successful cross country race is proper hydration. Dehydration can lead to poor performance, decreased energy levels, and even heat exhaustion, which can be dangerous. Therefore, it is crucial to hydrate properly before and during the race.

The first step to proper hydration is to start drinking water well before the race. Then, in the days leading up to the event, make sure you are consistently drinking water to keep your body hydrated. It is recommended to drink at least eight glasses of water per day.

On race day, start your hydration process by drinking water immediately after waking up. Make sure to continue drinking water leading up to the start of the race. A good rule of thumb is to consume 16 ounces of water 2-3 hours before the race and another 8-10 ounces about 20-30 minutes before the start.

During the race, make sure to take advantage of the water stations along the course. The general guideline is to drink 4-6 ounces of water every 20 minutes during the race to maintain hydration levels. However, this can vary depending on your individual needs and the temperature and humidity levels on race day.

It is important to note that hydration is not just about drinking water. Consuming electrolyte-rich drinks, such as sports drinks, can help maintain the proper balance of fluids in your body. Additionally, eating water-rich foods like fruits and vegetables can also contribute to proper hydration.

In conclusion, proper hydration is essential for successful cross country running. Starting the hydration process early, continuing to drink water leading up to the race, and taking advantage of water stations during the race can help you maintain the energy and focus needed to run your best race.

Tip 60: Eat a balanced meal: Eat a balanced meal that includes carbohydrates, protein, and healthy fats a few hours before the race to give your body the fuel it needs.

Eating a balanced meal a few hours before a cross country race can make a significant difference in your performance. The right combination of carbohydrates, protein, and healthy fats can provide the energy and nutrients your body needs to perform at its best.

Carbohydrates are the primary source of fuel for your muscles during exercise. Therefore, it is essential to consume enough carbohydrates to ensure that your body has enough energy to perform. Foods such as whole grains, fruits, and vegetables are excellent sources of carbohydrates and can help sustain energy levels throughout the race.

Protein is essential for muscle repair and growth, and it also helps regulate blood sugar levels, which is important during long-distance runs. Foods like eggs, lean meats, and legumes are excellent sources of protein and can help you feel fuller for longer.

Healthy fats are also essential for providing energy and can help sustain your energy levels during a race. Foods like nuts, seeds, and avocados are rich in healthy fats and can help you feel satisfied while also providing essential nutrients for your body.

It is important to note that each person's nutritional needs are different, and finding the right balance of nutrients that work for you may take some trial and error. Experimenting with different pre-race meal options during training can help you determine what foods work best for your body.

Additionally, timing is crucial when it comes to eating before a race. It is recommended to eat your pre-race meal 2-3 hours before the start of the race to give your body enough time to digest and absorb the nutrients.

In summary, consuming a balanced meal that includes carbohydrates, protein, and healthy fats a few hours before a cross country race can provide your body with the energy and nutrients it needs to perform at its best. Experimenting with different meal options during training and eating your pre-race meal at the right time can help you find the best nutritional strategy for your individual needs.

Tip 61: Avoid heavy or unfamiliar foods: Stick to familiar, easily digestible foods to avoid stomach upset or discomfort during the race.

When it comes to pre-race nutrition for cross country running, it is important to avoid heavy or unfamiliar foods that can cause stomach upset or discomfort during the race. Instead, it is recommended to stick to familiar, easily digestible foods to provide your body with the energy it needs without causing any gastrointestinal issues.

Heavy or greasy foods can take a long time to digest, causing discomfort and sluggishness during the race. These foods can also increase the risk of gastrointestinal distress, such as nausea or stomach cramps. Therefore, it is best to avoid these types of foods on race day.

Similarly, unfamiliar or exotic foods can be difficult for the body to digest, leading to discomfort and potential gastrointestinal issues. While trying new foods can be fun, it is best to save these culinary adventures for after the race.

To ensure that your body is fueled for the race without causing any digestive issues, stick to familiar, easily digestible foods. This can include options such as oatmeal with banana, toast with peanut butter, or a bagel with cream cheese. Other options could include a smoothie made with fruits and yogurt or a granola bar.

It is also important to consider the timing of your pre-race meal. Eating too close to the race can cause stomach upset, so it is recommended to eat your meal 2-3 hours before the start of the race to give your body enough time to digest.

In summary, to avoid stomach upset or discomfort during a cross country race, it is best to avoid heavy or unfamiliar foods and stick to familiar, easily digestible options. It is also important to eat your pre-race meal at the right time to give your body enough time to digest before the race.

Tip 62: Incorporate snacks: If you have a long wait between breakfast and the race, incorporate snacks such as fruit, energy bars, or sports drinks to keep your energy levels up.

If you have a long wait between breakfast and the start of your cross country race, it can be beneficial to incorporate snacks into your nutrition plan to keep your energy levels up. Snacks such as fruit, energy bars, or sports drinks can provide your body with the necessary fuel and hydration to perform at its best during the race.

Fruits such as bananas or apples can provide a quick source of energy and hydration due to their high water content and natural sugars. Energy bars or granola bars can provide a balance of carbohydrates, protein, and healthy fats, giving you sustained energy throughout the race. Look for bars that contain whole grains, nuts, and dried fruits, and avoid options that are high in added sugars.

Sports drinks are designed to provide your body with hydration and electrolytes, which can be especially important during longer races in hot and humid conditions. These drinks can also provide a quick source of carbohydrates for energy. However, be mindful of the sugar content in sports drinks and opt for options with lower sugar levels or make your own at home.

It is important to note that the timing of your snacks is crucial. Snacking too close to the race can cause stomach upset or cramping, so it is recommended to consume your snack at least 30-60 minutes before the start of the race. Additionally, be mindful of the type and number of snacks you consume. Too much food or too many high-sugar snacks can cause a sugar crash or digestive issues during the race.

In summary, incorporating snacks into your pre-race nutrition plan can be beneficial if you have a long wait between breakfast and the start of your cross country race. Fruits, energy bars, and sports drinks can provide your body with the necessary fuel and hydration to perform at its best during the race. However, be mindful of the type and number of snacks you consume; timing is crucial to avoid digestive issues during the race.

Tip 63: Be mindful of timing: Be mindful of the timing of your meals and snacks, making sure to eat early enough to allow for digestion before the race.

When it comes to pre-race nutrition for cross country running, timing is everything. It is essential to be mindful of the timing of your meals and snacks, making sure to eat early enough to allow for proper digestion before the race.

Eating too close to the start of the race can lead to discomfort, cramping, and other gastrointestinal issues. This is because digestion requires a significant amount of blood flow and energy, which can divert resources away from the muscles used during running. It is recommended to eat your meal or snack at least two to three hours before the race to avoid these issues.

If you are having a larger meal, such as breakfast or lunch, you should eat it three hours before the start of the race. This will allow your body enough time to digest the food and convert it into energy for your muscles. However, if you are eating a smaller snack, such as a granola bar or a banana, you can eat it closer to the start of the race, around 30 to 60 minutes before the race.

It is also important to be mindful of the type of food you are eating before the race. Foods high in fiber and fat can take longer to digest and can cause gastrointestinal distress, so it is best to avoid these types of foods before the race. Instead, opt for easily digestible foods rich in carbohydrates to give your body the energy it needs.

In summary, it is crucial to be mindful of the timing of your meals and snacks before a cross country race. Eating too close to the start of the race can cause discomfort and gastrointestinal issues. Aim to eat your meal or snack at least two to three hours before the race to allow for proper digestion. Also, be mindful of the type of food you are eating, and opt for easily digestible foods rich in carbohydrates.

Warm-Up Routine

Tip 64: Start with a light jog: Begin your warm-up with a light jog to get your blood flowing, and your muscles warmed up.

One of the key components of any successful cross country race is a proper warm-up routine. A good warm-up prepares your body for the physical demands of running by increasing blood flow to the muscles, raising body temperature, and improving flexibility. One great way to start your warm-up is with a light jog.

Starting with a light jog is an effective way to gradually increase your heart rate and get your muscles warmed up. This will help you avoid injuries and improve your overall performance during the race. A light jog is also a low-intensity exercise that will help your body transition from a resting state to a more active state.

Begin your jog at a slow and easy pace for around 5-10 minutes. You want to start at a pace that feels comfortable and allows you to breathe easily. As you continue to jog, gradually increase your pace and intensity, but make sure to avoid pushing yourself too hard too soon. The goal of this initial jog is to get your heart rate up and warm up your muscles gradually.

In addition to getting your blood flowing and muscles warmed up, starting with a light jog also has mental benefits. It can help you get into a focused and positive mindset before the race. It also gives you the opportunity to assess how your body is feeling and adjust your warm-up accordingly.

In summary, starting your warm-up routine with a light jog is an effective way to gradually increase your heart rate and warm up your muscles before a cross country race. Begin with a slow and easy pace for around 5-10 minutes, and gradually increase your intensity. This initial jog can help you avoid injuries, improve your performance, and get into a focused and positive mindset before the race.

Tip 65: Dynamic stretching: Incorporate dynamic stretching exercises, such as leg swings or high knees, to loosen up your muscles and joints.

Dynamic stretching is a crucial part of any warm-up routine for cross country running. Unlike static stretching, which involves holding a stretch for an extended period, dynamic stretching involves moving your joints and muscles through a range of motion. Incorporating dynamic stretching exercises before a race can help loosen up your muscles and joints, improve your flexibility, and reduce your risk of injury.

One effective dynamic stretching exercise is leg swings. To perform leg swings, stand with your feet shoulder-width apart and swing one leg forward and backward, keeping it straight while balancing on the opposite leg. Repeat this motion for 10-15 swings on each leg. This exercise helps to loosen up your hip flexors, glutes, and hamstrings, which are all important muscles for running.

Another great dynamic stretching exercise is high knees. To perform high knees, stand with your feet hip-width apart and lift one knee up towards your chest while hopping on the opposite foot. Repeat this motion, alternating legs, for 10-15 repetitions on each side. This exercise helps to warm up your hip flexors, quadriceps, and calves.

Incorporating dynamic stretching exercises into your warm-up routine can help you prepare your muscles and joints for the physical demands of running. By performing these exercises, you increase blood flow to your muscles and help reduce the risk of injury during the race.

It is important to note that dynamic stretching should not be confused with ballistic stretching, which involves bouncing or jerking movements. Ballistic stretching can cause muscle strain and is not recommended for warm-ups. Always make sure to perform dynamic stretching exercises in a controlled and safe manner.

In summary, incorporating dynamic stretching exercises, such as leg swings or high knees, into your warm-up routine can help loosen up your muscles and joints, improve flexibility, and reduce the risk of injury during a cross country race. These exercises are an effective way to prepare your body for the physical demands of running and should be performed in a controlled and safe manner.

Tip 66: Gradually increase intensity: As you warm up, gradually increase the intensity of your exercises to get your body ready for the race.

As mentioned earlier, a good warm-up routine is essential to prepare your body for the physical demands of cross country running. After starting with a light jog and incorporating dynamic stretching exercises, it's important to gradually increase the intensity of your warm-up to get your body fully prepared for the race.

As you progress through your warm-up routine, you can gradually increase the intensity of your exercises. For example, you can increase your jogging speed, add some hill sprints, or perform plyometric exercises such as jump squats or box jumps. These exercises will help elevate your heart rate and further warm up your muscles.

It's important to note that you should always increase the intensity of your warm-up gradually and at a pace that feels comfortable for you. Pushing yourself too hard too quickly can lead to injury and can also leave you feeling fatigued before the race even begins. As a general rule, you should aim to complete your warm-up routine about 10-15 minutes before the start of the race.

In addition to gradually increasing the intensity of your exercises, you can also incorporate some race-specific drills into your warm-up routine. For example, you can practice quick accelerations or short bursts of speed to help simulate the starts and surges that are common during a cross country race. This will help your body get used to the specific demands of the race and can also help you mentally prepare for the challenges ahead.

In summary, gradually increasing the intensity of your warm-up exercises is an important part of preparing your body for a cross country race. As you progress through your warm-up routine, you can increase your jogging speed, add in some hill sprints, or perform some plyometric exercises. It's important to increase the intensity gradually and at a pace that feels comfortable for you and to incorporate race-specific drills to help simulate the demands of the race. With a properly executed warm-up routine, you can help reduce the risk of injury and improve your overall performance during the race.

Tip 67: Practice strides: Do a few strides at a faster pace to get your body used to the speed of the race.

Strides are short, quick bursts of running at a faster pace than your warm-up jog. Practicing strides during your warm-up is an effective way to prepare your body for the increased speed of the race.

To perform strides, start with a slow jog, then gradually increase your pace over a short distance (around 80-100 meters) until you are running at close to your maximum speed. Hold that pace for a few seconds, then gradually slow back down to a jog. Repeat this process a few times, with short breaks between each stride.

By practicing strides, you are teaching your body to handle the faster pace of the race. Strides also help to improve your running form, as they encourage a more efficient stride pattern and promote good running posture. In addition, strides can help to reduce the risk of injury, as they warm up your muscles and joints even further, preparing them for the high-impact nature of running.

It's important to note that you should never push yourself to the point of exhaustion during strides, as this can increase your risk of injury and leave you feeling fatigued before the race even begins. Instead, focus on running at a comfortably fast pace and maintaining good form.

In summary, incorporating a few strides into your warm-up routine can be an effective way to prepare your body for the increased speed of the race. By practicing strides, you can improve your running form, reduce the risk of injury, and help your body handle the physical demands of cross country running.

Tip 68: Finish with a mental warm-up: Take a few minutes to mentally prepare for the race, visualizing your success and the feeling of accomplishment.

While physical preparation is crucial for cross country running, mental preparation is equally important. Taking a few minutes to warm up mentally before the race can help you feel more focused, confident, and prepared for the challenges ahead.

To perform a mental warm-up:

1. Find a quiet place where you can sit or stand comfortably.
2. Take a few deep breaths and clear your mind of any distractions or negative thoughts.
3. Visualize yourself successfully completing the race, crossing the finish line, and feeling a sense of accomplishment. You can also focus on specific goals you have for the race, such as finishing in a certain amount of time or passing a particular runner.

Positive self-talk can also be helpful during your mental warm-up. Repeat positive affirmations to yourself, such as "I am strong; I am capable; I am ready to run this race." This can help build your confidence and keep you motivated throughout the race.

In addition to visualization and positive self-talk, you can also use relaxation techniques such as progressive muscle relaxation or deep breathing to calm your nerves and reduce any pre-race anxiety.

Remember that everyone experiences pre-race nerves to some degree, and it's completely normal to feel a little bit nervous or excited before a big race. However, with a well-executed mental warm-up, you can channel those feelings into positive energy and focus, helping you perform your best on race day.

In summary, taking a few minutes to mentally prepare for the race can help you feel more focused, confident, and prepared for the challenges ahead. Visualization, positive self-talk, and relaxation techniques can all be helpful components of a mental warm-up routine. By combining physical and mental preparation, you can set yourself up for success and achieve your goals in cross country running.

Mental Preparation and Race Strategies

Tip 69: Set realistic goals: Set realistic goals for the race based on your current fitness level and past performance.

Setting realistic goals is an important part of preparing for a cross country race. Goals can help motivate you to train harder, stay focused during the race, and measure your progress over time. However, it's important to set goals that are challenging yet achievable based on your current fitness level and past performance.

To set realistic goals for your race, start by assessing your current fitness level. Consider how much training you've done leading up to the race, how well you've performed in previous races or workouts, and any injuries or limitations you may have. This will help you set a realistic baseline for your performance.

Next, consider the course and conditions of the race. Is it a hilly course or a flat course? Will you be running in hot or cold weather? These factors can impact your performance and should be taken into account when setting your goals.

Once you have a clear understanding of your fitness level and the conditions of the race, you can set goals that are challenging yet achievable. For example, if your best 5k time is 25 minutes, setting a goal of finishing the race in 20 minutes may be unrealistic. Instead, a more realistic goal may be to finish in 24 minutes or to improve your time by a certain percentage.

Remember to set both short-term and long-term goals. Short-term goals can help keep you motivated and focused on specific aspects of your training, while long-term goals can help guide your overall progress and development as a runner.

In summary, setting realistic goals is an important part of preparing for a cross country race. Assess your current fitness level, consider the course and conditions of the race, and set goals that are challenging yet achievable. By setting clear goals and tracking your progress, you can stay motivated and continue to improve as a cross country runner.

Tip 70: Focus on the process: Instead of solely focusing on the outcome of the race, focus on the process and what you can do to perform your best.

Focusing on the process is an important mindset to adopt when preparing for a cross country race. While it's natural to want to achieve a certain outcome, such as a personal best time or a high finish in the race, solely focusing on the outcome can cause unnecessary stress and pressure. By focusing on the process, you can take the pressure off the outcome and focus on what you can control to perform your best.

Focusing on the process means focusing on the day-to-day activities that lead up to the race, such as your training, nutrition, and mental preparation. This includes developing a training plan that focuses on building endurance, speed, and strength, as well as incorporating rest and recovery into your routine. It also means paying attention to your nutrition and hydration, as well as your mental state, and making adjustments as needed.

Another important aspect of focusing on the process is staying present in the moment during the race. Instead of thinking about the finish line or how far you have left to go, focus on your breathing, form, and pace. This can help you stay calm and focused and perform your best throughout the race.

By focusing on the process, you can also develop a growth mindset. This means embracing challenges and failures as opportunities for growth and learning rather than setbacks. This mindset can help you stay motivated and resilient throughout your training and racing and help you continue to improve over time.

In summary, focusing on the process is an important mindset to adopt when preparing for a cross country race. This means focusing on the day-to-day activities that lead up to the race, staying present during the race, and embracing challenges as opportunities for growth. By adopting a process-focused mindset, you can perform your best and continue to improve as a cross country runner.

Tip 71: Use positive self-talk: Use positive self-talk to stay motivated and confident throughout the race.

Positive self-talk is a powerful tool that can help you stay motivated and confident throughout a cross country race. It involves replacing negative thoughts or self-doubt with positive affirmations and encouragement.

During the race, it's common to experience negative thoughts, such as "I can't do this" or "I'm not fast enough." These thoughts can drain your energy and confidence and may even cause you to slow down or give up. By using positive self-talk, you can combat these negative thoughts and stay focused on your goals.

To use positive self-talk, start by identifying the negative thoughts that arise during the race. Then, replace them with positive affirmations and encouragement. For example, if you find yourself thinking, "I can't do this," replace it with, "I am strong and capable." Or if you're feeling discouraged, remind yourself of your training and preparation, saying something like, "I have worked hard for this, and I am ready."

It's also helpful to use positive self-talk to set goals and stay motivated during the race. For example, you might say to yourself,

"I am going to push through this hill," or "I will finish strong in the last mile." By setting small, achievable goals and using positive self-talk to stay motivated, you can maintain your focus and perform at your best.

In addition to helping you stay motivated, positive self-talk can also boost your confidence and improve your overall mood. When you speak to yourself in a positive and encouraging way, you'll feel more confident in your abilities and more optimistic about your performance.

In summary, using positive self-talk is an effective way to stay motivated and confident during a cross country race. By identifying negative thoughts and replacing them with positive affirmations and encouragement, you can combat self-doubt and stay focused on your goals.

Tip 72: Develop a race strategy: Plan your race strategy ahead of time, including how to approach hills and when to push yourself.

Developing a race strategy is an important step in achieving success in cross country running. A race strategy involves planning how you will approach the course, including hills, turns, and other obstacles. By developing a strategy ahead of time, you can conserve your energy, maintain a steady pace, and push yourself when needed.

To develop a race strategy, start by studying the course map and identifying any challenging sections, such as steep hills or sharp turns. Next, determine how you will approach these sections, such as slowing down or taking shorter strides on uphill sections.

It's also important to plan when you will push yourself during the race. For example, you might decide to pick up the pace during the second half of the race or to sprint to the finish line.

In addition to planning for the physical challenges of the race, it's also helpful to develop a mental strategy. For example, you might focus on staying positive and motivated throughout the race or on staying relaxed and maintaining good form.

Finally, it's important to remember that your race strategy may need to be adjusted based on race day conditions, such as weather or the performance of other runners. So remain flexible and be prepared to adapt your strategy if needed.

Overall, developing a race strategy is a key component of success in cross country running. By planning ahead and taking into account the course and your own abilities, you can run a smart, efficient race and achieve your goals.

Tip 73: Stay present and mindful: During the race, stay present and mindful, focusing on your breath and the rhythm of your steps to stay in the moment.

Staying present and mindful during a cross country race can help you maintain focus and perform at your best. It's easy to get distracted by the excitement of the race or the discomfort of pushing your body to its limits, but by practicing mindfulness, you can stay centered and focused.

One way to stay present is to focus on your breath. Take deep, controlled breaths, focusing on the sensation of the air moving in and out of your lungs. This can help you regulate your breathing and stay calm and centered.

Another way to stay present is to focus on the rhythm of your steps. Pay attention to the sound of your feet hitting the ground and the sensation of your body moving forward with each stride. This can help you maintain a steady pace and stay in the moment rather than worrying about the finish line or the competition.

It's also important to stay aware of your surroundings during the race, such as other runners and any obstacles on the course.

However, try not to get too caught up in external distractions. Instead, stay focused on your own performance and your own goals.

Finally, remember to stay positive and use positive self-talk throughout the race. Remind yourself of your strengths and capabilities, and focus on the progress you are making rather than any setbacks or challenges you may encounter.

By staying present and mindful during a cross country race, you can maintain focus and perform at your best, achieving your goals and feeling accomplished at the finish line.

Chapter Review

- Proper hydration and nutrition are essential before a cross country race to fuel your body and prevent discomfort or stomach upset.
- Incorporating snacks can help maintain energy levels during long wait times between meals and the race start.
- A proper warm-up should include a light jog, dynamic stretching exercises, strides, and mental preparation.
- Staying present and mindful during the race can help maintain focus and avoid distractions, such as external competitors or obstacles on the course.
- Using positive self-talk and focusing on the process rather than just the outcome can help build confidence and motivation during the race.

Chapter 6: Injury Prevention and Recovery

Common Running Injuries

Tip 74: Runner's Knee: This is a common overuse injury that occurs when the cartilage on the underside of the kneecap wears away. It can cause pain and swelling around the kneecap.

As a cross country runner, one of the most frustrating things that can happen to you is developing an injury that prevents you from running. Runner's knee is a common overuse injury that plagues many runners, but the good news is that it is preventable and treatable.

The knee joint is made up of three bones: the femur, the tibia, and the patella (kneecap). The patella is covered in a layer of cartilage that helps it glide smoothly over the other bones. When this cartilage wears away due to repetitive stress from running, it can cause pain and swelling around the kneecap, known as the runner's knee.

It is important to take good care of your knees to prevent runner's knee. This includes warming up properly before running, wearing the right shoes, and gradually increasing your mileage. Strengthening exercises for the muscles around your knee, such as your quadriceps and hamstrings, can also help prevent injury.

If you do develop runner's knee, the first step is to rest and avoid running until the pain subsides. Ice and anti-inflammatory medication can help reduce swelling and pain. Physical therapy exercises such as stretching and strengthening can also help rehabilitate the knee.

In summary, runner's knee is a common injury that can be prevented and treated. By taking good care of your knees and listening to your body, you can continue to enjoy running and avoid injury.

Tip 75: Shin Splints: This injury causes pain along the inside or outside of the shinbone. It's often caused by overuse or a sudden increase in training volume.

Shin splints are a painful and common injury among cross country runners. They are often caused by overuse or a sudden increase in training volume. If left untreated, shin splints can develop into more serious injuries that may require more extensive treatment.

The shinbone, or tibia, is one of the major bones in the lower leg. It is surrounded by muscles that are attached to it by a tough layer of tissue called the periosteum. When these muscles are overworked, they can cause tiny tears in the periosteum, leading to pain and inflammation along the inside or outside of the shinbone.

To prevent shin splints, it's important to gradually increase your training volume and intensity. Warming up properly before each run and stretching your calves and shins can also help prevent injury. Wearing shoes with good shock absorption and support can also help reduce the impact on your shins.

If you do develop shin splints, the first step is to rest and avoid running until the pain subsides. Ice and anti-inflammatory medication can help reduce swelling and pain. Physical therapy exercises such as strengthening and stretching can also help rehabilitate the shin.

In summary, shin splints are a common injury among cross country runners that can be prevented by taking the necessary precautions and gradually increasing your training volume. However, if you do develop shin splints, it's important to take prompt action and allow your body to rest and heal before returning to running.

Tip 76: IT Band Syndrome: The IT (iliotibial) band is a thick band of tissue that runs along the outside of the thigh. When it becomes inflamed, it can cause pain on the outside of the knee.

IT band syndrome is a painful injury that affects many runners, especially those who run long distances. The IT band is a thick band of tissue that runs along the outside of the thigh and connects the hip to the knee. When this band becomes inflamed or tight, it can cause pain on the outside of the knee.

IT band syndrome is often caused by overuse, improper running form, or weak hip muscles. It can also be caused by wearing shoes that are worn out or do not provide proper support. Symptoms of IT band syndrome may include pain or tenderness on the outside of the knee, swelling, or a snapping sensation when bending or extending the knee.

To prevent IT band syndrome, it's important to gradually increase your training volume and ensure that you are using the proper running form. Stretching your IT band and hip muscles, as well as using foam rollers or massage balls to release tension, can also help prevent injury.

If you do develop IT band syndrome, it's important to rest and avoid activities that exacerbate the pain. Ice and anti-inflammatory medication can help reduce swelling and pain. Physical therapy exercises such as stretching and strengthening can also help rehabilitate the IT band.

In summary, IT band syndrome is a common injury among runners that can be prevented by taking the necessary precautions and ensuring that you are using the proper running form. If you do develop IT band syndrome, it's important to take prompt action and allow your body to rest and heal before returning to running.

Tip 77: Plantar Fasciitis: This is an inflammation of the plantar fascia, a thick band of tissue that runs along the bottom of the foot. It can cause heel pain and stiffness.

Plantar fasciitis is a common injury among runners, and it can be a frustrating and painful condition to deal with. The plantar fascia is a thick band of tissue that runs along the bottom of the foot, connecting the heel bone to the toes. When this tissue becomes inflamed, it can cause sharp pain in the heel or arch of the foot, especially when you first get out of bed in the morning.

One of the most common causes of plantar fasciitis in runners is overuse. When you run or walk long distances, the repetitive impact can put a lot of strain on the plantar fascia. In addition, tight calf muscles, flat feet, or high arches can also contribute to the development of plantar fasciitis.

If you think you have plantar fasciitis, it's important to seek treatment as soon as possible. Ignoring the pain or continuing to run through the injury can make it worse and prolong the healing process. Here are some tips for treating plantar fasciitis:

Rest: Give your foot time to rest and heal. Avoid activities that exacerbate the pain, such as running or jumping.

Ice: Applying ice to the affected area can help reduce inflammation and relieve pain. Ice your foot for 15-20 minutes at a time, several times a day.

Stretch: Stretching your calf muscles and the bottom of your foot can help reduce tension and relieve pain. Try doing calf stretches, toe curls, and rolling a golf ball under your foot.

Support: Wearing shoes with good arch support can help take pressure off the plantar fascia. Consider getting custom orthotics to provide additional support and cushioning.

Physical therapy: Working with a physical therapist can help you develop a treatment plan and learn exercises to strengthen your foot and prevent future injuries.

With proper treatment and rest, most cases of plantar fasciitis can be successfully treated within a few weeks to a few months. However, it's important to take steps to prevent it from coming back by wearing proper footwear, stretching regularly, and gradually increasing your training volume.

Stretching and Mobility Exercises

Tip 78: Hip Flexor Stretch: Kneel on one knee with your other leg in front of you, your foot flat on the ground. Lean forward into the stretch, feeling a stretch in your hip flexors. Hold for 30 seconds and repeat on the other side.

The hip flexor stretch is a simple but effective exercise that can help prevent injuries and improve performance in cross country running. This stretch targets the hip flexor muscles responsible for lifting your legs during running.

To perform the hip flexor stretch, kneel on one knee with your other leg in front of you, your foot flat on the ground. Your front knee should be bent at a 90-degree angle. Keeping your back straight, gently lean forward into the stretch, feeling a stretch in your hip flexors. Hold the stretch for 30 seconds, and then repeat on the other side.

It's important to perform this stretch regularly, especially if you sit for long periods of time or have tight hip flexor muscles. By stretching these muscles, you can improve your range of motion and reduce your risk of injury.

In addition to the hip flexor stretch, there are several other exercises and stretches that can help prevent injuries and improve performance in cross country running. Strengthening exercises for the hip and glute muscles, such as squats and lunges, can help improve your running form and prevent injuries. Stretching exercises for the calves, hamstrings, and IT band can also help improve flexibility and reduce your risk of injury.

In summary, the hip flexor stretch is a simple but effective exercise that can help prevent injuries and improve performance in cross country running. By incorporating this stretch, as well as other strengthening and stretching exercises, into your training routine, you can improve your overall fitness and become a better runner.

Tip 79: Calf Stretch: Stand facing a wall with your hands on the wall at shoulder height. Step one foot back, keeping your heel on the ground, and lean forward into the stretch. Hold for 30 seconds and repeat on the other side.

The calf stretch is a classic exercise that can help prevent injuries and improve performance in cross country running. This stretch targets the calf muscles, which are responsible for pushing off the ground during running.

To perform the calf stretch, stand facing a wall with your hands on the wall at shoulder height. Step one foot back, keeping your heel on the ground. Your front foot should be flat on the ground with your knee bent. Gently lean forward into the stretch, feeling a stretch in your calf muscle. Hold the stretch for 30 seconds, and then repeat on the other side.

It's important to perform this stretch regularly, especially if you have tight calf muscles. By stretching these muscles, you can improve your range of motion and reduce your risk of injury.

In addition to the calf stretch, there are several other exercises and stretches that can help prevent injuries and improve performance in cross country running. Strengthening exercises for the ankle and foot muscles, such as toe raises and ankle circles, can help improve your running form and prevent injuries. Stretching exercises for the hamstrings, hip flexors, and IT band can also help improve flexibility and reduce your risk of injury.

In summary, the calf stretch is a simple but effective exercise that can help prevent injuries and improve performance in cross country running. By incorporating this stretch, as well as other strengthening and stretching exercises, into your training routine, you can improve your overall fitness and become a better runner.

Tip 80: Foam Rolling: Foam rolling can help release tight muscles and increase mobility. Roll your muscles over a foam roller, focusing on any areas that feel tight or sore.

Foam rolling is a popular self-myofascial release technique that can help prevent injuries and improve performance in cross country running. This technique involves using a foam roller to apply pressure to your muscles, helping to release tightness and increase mobility.

To perform foam rolling, lie down on your side and place the foam roller under your hip. Then, roll your body over the foam roller, focusing on any areas that feel tight or sore. You can also target specific muscles, such as your quads, hamstrings, and calves, by rolling them over the foam roller.

It's important to use proper technique when foam rolling to avoid causing injury. Start by applying light pressure and gradually increase the pressure as your muscles become more relaxed. Be sure to avoid rolling over any bony areas, which can cause pain and discomfort.

Foam rolling can be done before or after a workout or as a standalone activity. It can help improve your range of motion, reduce muscle soreness, and prevent injuries. Incorporating foam rolling into your regular training routine can help you become a better runner and improve your overall fitness.

In addition to foam rolling, there are several other techniques and exercises that can help prevent injuries and improve performance in cross country running. Stretching, strengthening exercises, and proper running form are all important components of a well-rounded training routine.

In summary, foam rolling is a simple but effective technique that can help prevent injuries and improve performance in cross country running. By incorporating foam rolling, as well as other techniques and exercises, into your training routine, you can improve your overall fitness and become a better runner.

Proper Recovery Techniques

Tip 81: Rest and Ice: Resting the injured area and applying ice can help reduce swelling and speed up the healing process.

Rest and ice are important components of injury management in cross country running. When you experience an injury, it's important to give your body time to rest and heal. Applying ice to the injured area can also help reduce swelling and speed up the healing process.

To use rest and ice as a treatment for an injury, start by resting the injured area as much as possible. This means avoiding any activities that could aggravate the injury and taking a break from your regular training routine. Depending on the severity of the injury, you may need to rest for several days or weeks.

In addition to resting, applying ice to the injured area can help reduce inflammation and promote healing. To use ice as a treatment, wrap an ice pack or a bag of ice in a towel and apply it to the injured area for 20 minutes at a time. You can repeat this several times a day, as needed.

It's important to note that while rest and ice can be effective treatments for injuries, they should not be used as a substitute for proper medical care. If you have a serious injury or are experiencing severe pain, it's important to seek medical attention from a qualified healthcare professional.

In addition to rest and ice, there are several other treatments and techniques that can help prevent injuries and improve performance in cross country running. Proper warm-up and cool-down routines, stretching and strengthening exercises, and proper running form are all important components of injury prevention and management.

In summary, rest and ice are important components of injury management in cross country running. By incorporating these techniques, as well as other treatments and techniques, into your training routine, you can help prevent injuries and improve your overall performance. If you do experience an injury, be sure to seek medical attention and follow a proper treatment plan to ensure a full and speedy recovery.

Tip 82: Compression: Compression can help reduce swelling and provide support to the injured area. You can use compression socks or wraps.

Compression is a popular treatment technique used in cross country running to help reduce swelling and provide support to injured areas. Compression works by applying pressure to the injured area, which helps to increase blood flow and reduce inflammation.

There are several ways to apply compression, including using compression socks, compression sleeves, or compression wraps. Compression socks and sleeves are designed to be worn on the legs and provide continuous compression to the calves and shins. Compression wraps, on the other hand, can be applied directly to the injured area, such as the ankle or knee.

To use compression as a treatment for an injury, start by choosing the appropriate type of compression garment. Compression socks and sleeves are typically made of a tight, stretchy material that provides graduated compression. The pressure is highest at the ankle and decreases as it moves up the leg. Compression wraps, on the other hand, can be adjusted to provide the desired level of compression.

Once you have the appropriate compression garment, apply it to the injured area as directed. Compression garments can be worn during activity or while resting, depending on the severity of the injury and the recommendation of your healthcare provider.

In addition to providing support and reducing swelling, compression can also help prevent injuries by improving circulation and reducing muscle fatigue. Many athletes wear compression garments during training and competition to improve their performance and reduce their risk of injury.

In summary, compression is a popular treatment technique used in cross country running to help reduce swelling and provide support to injured areas. By using compression socks, sleeves, or wraps, you can help promote healing and prevent future injuries. Be sure to choose the appropriate type of compression garment and follow the recommended guidelines for use to ensure optimal results.

Tip 83: Elevation: Elevating the injured area above your heart can also help reduce swelling.

Elevating the injured area is another effective technique used in cross country running to help reduce swelling and promote healing. Elevating the injured area above the level of your heart can help to reduce the amount of blood flow to the area, which in turn helps to reduce swelling and inflammation.

To use elevation as a treatment for an injury, start by finding a comfortable position where you can elevate the injured area above your heart. For example, if you have a knee injury, you can lie on your back with your leg propped up on pillows or a chair. If you have a foot or ankle injury, you can sit in a chair and prop your foot up on another chair or a footstool.

Once you have the injured area elevated, try to keep it in this position for at least 20 to 30 minutes at a time, several times a day. You can also try to elevate the injured area while you sleep by propping it up with pillows.

In addition to reducing swelling and promoting healing, elevation can also help to relieve pain and discomfort associated with the injury. By reducing swelling and inflammation, elevation can help to improve your range of motion and flexibility, allowing you to return to your regular training routine more quickly.

It's important to note that while elevation can be an effective treatment technique for injuries, it should be used in conjunction with other treatments and techniques, such as rest, ice, compression, and proper medical care. If you have a serious injury or are experiencing severe pain, it's important to seek medical attention from a qualified healthcare professional.

In summary, elevation is an effective technique used in cross country running to help reduce swelling and promote healing. By elevating the injured area above your heart several times a day, you can reduce inflammation, relieve pain, and improve your range of motion and flexibility. Incorporate elevation into your injury management plan, along with other techniques such as rest, ice, compression, and proper medical care, to ensure a full and speedy recovery.

Tip 84: Cross-Training: If you're injured, it's important to stay active to maintain your fitness. Consider cross-training activities like swimming or cycling that are low-impact and won't aggravate your injury.

Cross-training is an excellent way to stay active and maintain your fitness level when you're unable to run due to injury. Cross-training activities like swimming, cycling, or using an elliptical machine are low-impact and won't aggravate your injury, allowing you to stay active while you recover.

Cross-training can also help to prevent injury by strengthening different muscle groups and improving overall fitness. By incorporating different activities into your routine, you can reduce the risk of overuse injuries and improve your performance on the cross country course.

When choosing a cross-training activity, it's important to choose an activity that is low-impact and won't aggravate your injury. For example, swimming is an excellent choice because it's low-impact and provides a full-body workout. Cycling is also a good option because it's low-impact and can be done indoors or outdoors, depending on your preference.

Elliptical machines are another popular cross-training option because they provide a low-impact, full-body workout that simulates running without the impact on your joints. Yoga and Pilates can also be effective cross-training activities because they improve flexibility, balance, and core strength.

When incorporating cross-training into your routine, it's important to listen to your body and not overdo it. Start with shorter sessions and gradually increase the duration and intensity as your fitness level improves. Remember also to incorporate rest days into your routine to allow your body to recover and prevent overuse injuries.

In summary, cross-training is an effective way to maintain your fitness level when you're unable to run due to injury. First, choose low-impact activities like swimming, cycling, or using an elliptical machine that won't aggravate your injury. Then, incorporate cross-training into your routine gradually and listen to your body to avoid overuse injuries. By staying active and incorporating different activities into your routine, you can improve your performance on the cross country course and reduce the risk of injury.

Tip 85: Physical Therapy: If your injury is severe, working with a physical therapist can help you recover and prevent future injuries.

If you've suffered a severe injury, working with a physical therapist can be essential for your recovery and for preventing future injuries. Physical therapy is a form of rehabilitation that involves exercises, manual therapy, and other techniques to help you regain strength, flexibility, and range of motion.

A physical therapist will work with you to develop a personalized treatment plan that addresses your specific injury and goals. They may use exercises to help you regain strength and flexibility in the injured area, as well as manual therapy techniques like massage or stretching to improve mobility and reduce pain.

In addition to helping you recover from your injury, physical therapy can also help prevent future injuries. A physical therapist can assess your running form and identify any imbalances or weaknesses that may increase your risk of injury. They can then develop a targeted exercise program to address these issues and help you run more efficiently and with less risk of injury.

Physical therapy can also help you learn how to properly warm up and cool down before and after running, as well as how to stretch and foam roll effectively. These techniques can help reduce muscle tightness and soreness, which can also help prevent future injuries.

If you're considering physical therapy, talk to your doctor or healthcare provider. They can help you find a qualified physical therapist in your area who specializes in sports injuries and can help you get back on the road to recovery. By working with a physical therapist, you can regain your strength, prevent future injuries, and get back to running at your best.

Tips for Preventing Injuries

Tip 86: Gradually Increase Training Volume: Avoid sudden increases in training volume, which can put you at risk for injury.

One of the most important tips for avoiding injury in cross country running is to increase your training volume gradually. This means you should increase the distance, intensity, or duration of your runs slowly over time rather than making sudden jumps.

Sudden increases in training volume can put a lot of stress on your body, increasing your risk of injury. Your muscles, bones, and connective tissues need time to adapt to the demands of running, and pushing too hard too quickly can cause damage and inflammation.

To avoid injury, aim to increase your training volume by no more than 10% per week. This means that if you're currently running 20 miles per week, you should aim to increase your weekly mileage to no more than 22 miles the following week.

It's also important to listen to your body and adjust your training plan as needed. If you're feeling particularly fatigued or sore, take a rest day or reduce the intensity of your workout. Pushing through pain or fatigue can increase your risk of injury and set back your training progress.

By gradually increasing your training volume and listening to your body, you can stay injury-free and enjoy the many benefits of cross country running.

Tip 87: Wear Proper Shoes: Make sure you're wearing shoes that are appropriate for your foot type and running style.

Wearing proper shoes is crucial for preventing injury in cross country running. The right shoes will provide support and cushioning where you need it most and can help correct any imbalances or abnormalities in your foot or gait.

When choosing running shoes, it's important to consider your foot type and running style. There are three basic types of feet: flat, neutral, and high-arched. Each type of foot requires a different type of shoe to provide the right amount of support and cushioning.

Flat feet tend to overpronate or roll inward when running, so runners with flat feet should look for shoes with good arch support and stability. Neutral feet have a natural, even stride, so runners with neutral feet can generally choose a shoe with moderate support and cushioning. High-arched feet tend to underpronate or roll outward when running, so runners with high arches should look for shoes with good cushioning and flexibility.

In addition to considering your foot type, it's also important to consider your running style. Some runners land on their heel, while others land on the ball of their foot or midfoot. Different shoes are designed to provide cushioning and support for different types of foot strikes.

To ensure that you're wearing the right shoes for your foot type and running style, it's a good idea to visit a specialty running store and have your feet measured and gait analyzed. Then, a trained professional can help you choose the right shoes for your needs and ensure you're running safely and comfortably.

By wearing proper shoes, you can reduce your risk of injury and enjoy a more comfortable, efficient run.

Tip 88: Listen to Your Body: Pay attention to any aches or pains and address them before they turn into injuries. Rest when you need to, and don't push through the pain.

Listening to your body is key to preventing injuries in cross country running. When you push yourself too hard, ignore warning signs, or don't give your body the rest it needs, you put yourself at risk for injury.

Pay attention to any aches or pains, no matter how minor they may seem. Address them early on before they become more serious injuries. If you feel a twinge in your knee or your ankle starts to ache, take a break from running and give your body time to rest and recover. Ignoring pain or discomfort and continuing to run can lead to more serious injuries down the road.

Rest is an important part of any training program, and it's especially important when you're trying to prevent injuries. When you feel tired or run down, take a day off from running and focus on recovery. Make sure you're getting enough sleep, eating a healthy diet, and giving your body time to heal between runs.

It's also important to avoid pushing through pain. While it's normal to experience some discomfort during a hard workout, persistent pain is a sign that something is wrong. Continuing to run when you're in pain can exacerbate the injury and make it worse.

In summary, listening to your body is one of the most important things you can do to prevent injuries in cross country running. By paying attention to warning signs, taking time to rest and recover, and avoiding pushing through pain, you can stay healthy and injury-free as you pursue your running goals.

Chapter Review

- Cross country runners are prone to several injuries, including runner's knee, shin splints, IT band syndrome, and plantar fasciitis.
- It's important to take steps to prevent injuries, such as wearing proper shoes, gradually increasing training volume, and listening to your body.
- In the event of an injury, rest, ice, compression, and elevation can help reduce swelling and speed up the healing process.
- Stretching and foam rolling can help release tight muscles and increase mobility, while cross-training activities can help you maintain your fitness while recovering from an injury.
- If your injury is severe, working with a physical therapist can help you recover and prevent future injuries.

Chapter 7: Staying Motivated and Moving Forward

Maintaining Motivation Throughout Training

Tip 89: Mix up your routes: Running the same route day after day can become monotonous. Switch up your scenery and explore new trails or paths to keep things interesting.

As a seasoned cross country runner, I've learned that one of the most important things you can do to keep your training fresh is to mix up your routes. It's easy to fall into the trap of running the same course day after day, but doing so can lead to boredom and a lack of motivation. Instead, try exploring new trails or paths to keep things interesting.

Not only will changing up your routes help keep you mentally engaged, but it can also have physical benefits. Running on different surfaces and terrains can challenge your body in new ways, working different muscles and helping to prevent overuse injuries.

When selecting new routes, consider the terrain and elevation changes. Running uphill or downhill requires different muscle groups than running on flat ground. Incorporating hills into your training can improve your overall strength and endurance, making you a stronger runner.

Another benefit of mixing up your routes is that it can help you avoid burnout. Running the same route day after day can become monotonous, leading to a lack of motivation and a plateau in your performance. By exploring new trails and paths, you'll keep things fresh and exciting, which can help you stay motivated and focused on your goals.

In summary, mixing up your routes is a simple but effective tip for any cross country runner looking to improve their performance and stay motivated. By exploring new trails and paths, you'll challenge your body in new ways, prevent burnout, and keep your training fresh and exciting. So the next time you head out for a run, try a new route and see how it can impact your training.

Tip 90: Try new workout types: Incorporate different types of workouts into your routine, such as hill repeats, tempo runs, and interval training, to challenge your body in different ways.

As a cross country runner, it's important to challenge your body in different ways to improve your overall performance. One way to do this is by incorporating different types of workouts into your routine. Adding workouts such as hill repeats, tempo runs, and interval training can help you build strength, endurance, and speed.

Hill repeats are an effective way to build leg strength and improve your running form. Find a hill that's challenging but still manageable, and run up it at a steady pace. Once you reach the top, jog or walk back down, and repeat the process several times. Hill repeats are great for building power and improving your overall endurance.

Tempo runs are another way to improve your running performance. During a tempo run, you maintain a steady pace that's slightly faster than your usual pace for an extended period of time. This type of workout helps your body learn to tolerate a higher level of lactic acid, which can lead to increased endurance and faster race times.

Interval training is a type of workout that involves short bursts of high-intensity running followed by a period of rest. For example, you might run at your maximum effort for 30 seconds, followed by a minute of rest, and repeat the process several times. Interval training can help improve your speed and cardiovascular endurance.

Incorporating different types of workouts into your routine can help you break through plateaus and reach new levels of performance. It's important to remember to gradually increase the intensity and volume of your workouts to avoid injury.

In summary, trying new workout types is a great way to challenge your body in different ways and improve your cross country running performance. Hill repeats, tempo runs, and interval training are just a few examples of workouts that can help you build strength, endurance, and speed. By incorporating these workouts into your routine, you'll be on your way to becoming a stronger, faster runner.

Tip 91: Keep a training log: Tracking your workouts can help you see your progress and stay motivated. Plus, looking back at your accomplishments can be a great way to boost your confidence.

Keeping a training log is an essential tool for any serious cross country runner. Not only can it help you track your progress, but it can also help you stay motivated and hold yourself accountable. Here are some tips for starting and maintaining a training log:

First, decide on a format that works for you. Some runners prefer to use a traditional paper journal, while others use digital apps or spreadsheets. Choose a format that you'll enjoy using, and that will be easy for you to maintain.

Next, set up your training log. Include the date, the type of workout you completed (such as an easy run, interval workout, or tempo run), the distance you covered, and any notes about how you felt during the workout.

As you progress in your training, make sure to include other important details, such as the time it took you to complete the workout, your heart rate, or any other factors that may have impacted your performance.

Regularly reviewing your training log can help you see patterns and trends in your training, such as which types of workouts are most effective for you or when you need to adjust your training to avoid injury or burnout.

Perhaps most importantly, keeping a training log can help boost your motivation and confidence. Seeing how far you've come and how much progress you've made can help you stay focused on your goals and remind you of what you're capable of achieving.

In summary, keeping a training log is a simple but powerful way to track your progress, stay motivated, and boost your confidence as a cross country runner. By setting up a log that works for you and regularly reviewing your progress, you'll be on your way to reaching your goals and becoming a stronger, faster runner.

Accountability Partners and Teams

Tip 92: Join a running club: Running with a group can provide accountability, support, and motivation. Plus, it's a great way to meet new people who share your passion for running.

Joining a running club can be a great way to enhance your cross country running experience. Running with a group provides many benefits, including accountability, support, and motivation. Here are some reasons why you should consider joining a running club:

First, running with a group provides accountability. When you know that others are expecting you to show up for a group run, it can be easier to stay committed to your training. Having a regular schedule of group runs can also help you establish a consistent routine, which is key to achieving your running goals.

Second, joining a running club provides support. Running can be a challenging and sometimes lonely sport, but when you run with a group, you have others who understand the ups and downs of training. You can share tips, encouragement, and advice and celebrate each other's successes.

Third, running with a group provides motivation. When you see other runners pushing themselves and achieving their goals, it can be inspiring and motivating. Plus, when you run with others, you can challenge yourself to keep up with the group, which can help you push past your own limits and achieve new levels of performance.

Finally, joining a running club is a great way to meet new people who share your passion for running. You can make new friends, connect with others who have similar goals, and even learn about new races or training opportunities.

In summary, joining a running club is a fantastic way to enhance your cross country running experience. By running with a group, you can gain accountability, support, and motivation and meet new people who share your passion for running. So why not find a local running club and join in on the fun?

Tip 93: Find a running buddy: Having a running partner can help keep you accountable and make your training more enjoyable. Plus, it's always more fun to have someone to chat with during a long run.

Having a running buddy is a great way to stay motivated and accountable and make your training more enjoyable. Running with a partner can help you push yourself harder, stay focused on your goals, and even make the time fly by during long runs. Here are some tips for finding a running buddy:

First, consider your training goals and running pace. Look for someone who has similar goals and fitness levels to you, so you can both benefit from each other's training. You can find running partners through social media groups, local running clubs, or even by asking around among friends and family.

Second, set up a regular running schedule with your partner. Consistency is key to achieving your goals, so try to find a schedule that works for both of you and stick to it. This will help you stay accountable to each other and make sure that you're both making progress toward your goals.

Third, make sure to communicate your expectations and boundaries with your running partner. For example, if you prefer to run in the morning, make sure your partner is aware of that. If you need to take a rest day, communicate that with your partner in advance.

Fourth, make running fun! Plan routes that you both enjoy, mix up your workouts, and consider signing up for a race or virtual event together. By making running enjoyable and social, you'll both be more likely to stick with it and achieve your goals.

In summary, finding a running buddy can be a great way to enhance your cross country running experience. By choosing a compatible partner, setting up a regular schedule, communicating clearly, and making running fun, you can stay motivated and accountable, and make new friends along the way. So, reach out to a potential running partner today and start enjoying the many benefits of running with a buddy!

Tip 94: Sign up for a race: Registering for a race can give you a concrete goal to work towards and provide a sense of accountability.

Signing up for a race can be a great way to stay motivated and focused on your cross country running goals. By registering for a race, you'll have a concrete goal to work towards, which can provide a sense of purpose and accountability. Here are some tips for choosing and preparing for a race:

First, choose a race that aligns with your fitness level and training goals. Consider factors such as distance, terrain, and location when selecting a race. Make sure that you have enough time to train for the race and that you're realistic about your ability to complete the distance.

Second, create a training plan that prepares you for the race. Your training plan should include a mix of running, cross-training, and rest days and should gradually increase in intensity as you get closer to the race. Consider working with a coach or personal trainer to develop a personalized training plan that meets your specific needs.

Third, stay focused on your race goals throughout your training. Keep a positive attitude, stay motivated, and celebrate your progress along the way. Consider tracking your progress in a training log or journal to help you stay on track and motivated.

Fourth, prepare for race day by familiarizing yourself with the course, checking the weather forecast, and getting plenty of rest the night before. Finally, make sure that you have all the necessary gear, such as running shoes, hydration, and nutrition, and plan to arrive at the race early to avoid last-minute stress.

In summary, signing up for a race can be a great way to stay motivated and focused on your cross country running goals. By choosing a race that aligns with your fitness level and training goals, creating a training plan, staying focused on your goals, and preparing for race day, you can achieve success and enjoy the many benefits of cross country running. So, sign up for a race today and start working towards your next running goal!

Celebrating Your Progress and Setting New Goals

Tip 95: Take progress photos: Snap photos of yourself throughout your training and compare them to see how far you've come. Celebrate the progress you've made and use it as motivation to keep going.

Taking progress photos is a great way to track your progress and see how far you've come in your cross country running journey. Not only can it be motivating to see the changes in your body, but it can also be a helpful tool to track your running form and technique. Here are some tips for taking progress photos:

First, establish a regular schedule for taking photos. This could be weekly, bi-weekly, or monthly depending on your preference. Make sure to take the photos in the same location and under the same conditions each time, such as in the morning before a run.

Second, wear the same or similar clothing in each photo. This will help you to better compare your progress and see the changes in your body.

Third, take photos from multiple angles, including front, back, and side views. This will give you a more complete picture of your progress and help you to track changes in your posture and form.

Fourth, celebrate your progress! Comparing your photos over time can be a powerful motivator to keep going, even when progress seems slow. Celebrate the changes you've made and use them as a reminder of why you started in the first place.

In summary, taking progress photos can be a great tool to track your progress and see how far you've come in your cross country running journey. By establishing a regular schedule, wearing similar clothing, taking photos from multiple angles, and celebrating your progress, you can use your progress photos as a powerful motivator to keep pushing yourself toward your running goals. So, grab your camera and start documenting your progress today!

Tip 96: Treat yourself: When you hit a major milestone, like running your first 10K or completing a difficult workout, treat yourself to something special. It doesn't have to be a big reward, just something that makes you happy and proud of yourself.

Treating yourself can be a great way to stay motivated and reward yourself for your hard work and dedication in cross country running. When you hit a major milestone, such as completing a difficult workout or achieving a personal record, taking time to celebrate your accomplishment can help you stay motivated and focused on your goals. Here are some tips for treating yourself:

First, choose a reward that aligns with your values and goals. For example, if you're trying to eat healthier, treat yourself to a healthy meal or snack. If you're trying to save money, choose a reward that doesn't break the bank, such as a movie night at home or a relaxing bath.

Second, make sure that your reward is something that you truly enjoy and look forward to. It should be something that brings you joy and makes you proud of your accomplishments.

Third, use your reward as a way to acknowledge your hard work and dedication. Celebrate your progress and use it as motivation to keep going.

Fourth, don't be afraid to share your accomplishment and reward with others. Sharing your success can help to keep you accountable and motivated and can also inspire others to pursue their own goals.

In summary, treating yourself can be a great way to stay motivated and celebrate your accomplishments in cross country running. By choosing a reward that aligns with your values and goals, choosing something you enjoy, using your reward to acknowledge your hard work and dedication, and sharing your accomplishment with others, you can stay motivated and focused on your goals. So, go ahead and treat yourself when you hit a major milestone – you deserve it!

Tip 97: Set realistic goals: Setting goals that are challenging but attainable can help you stay motivated and make progress. Make sure to set both short-term and long-term goals.

Setting realistic goals is key to making progress in cross country running. Goals that are challenging yet attainable can help keep you motivated and focused on your training. Here are some tips for setting realistic goals:

First, start by setting both short-term and long-term goals. Short-term goals could be something like running a certain distance or completing a specific workout, while long-term goals could be completing a race or improving your overall pace.

Second, make sure that your goals are specific and measurable. For example, instead of setting a goal to "get better at running," set a goal to improve your 5K time by a certain amount.

Third, consider setting goals that are based on effort rather than outcome. This means setting a goal to complete a certain number of workouts each week or to run for a certain amount of time each day rather than focusing solely on your pace or distance.

Fourth, make sure that your goals are realistic and attainable. It's important to challenge yourself, but setting goals that are too difficult or unrealistic can be demotivating.

Fifth, track your progress toward your goals. This could mean using a running app to track your pace and distance or keeping a training log to record your workouts.

Finally, celebrate your progress along the way. Each time you reach a milestone or achieve a goal, take time to acknowledge your hard work and dedication.

In summary, setting realistic goals is key to making progress in cross country running. By setting both short-term and long-term goals, making sure that they are specific and measurable, focusing on effort rather than outcome, making sure that they are realistic and attainable, tracking your progress, and celebrating your progress along the way, you can stay motivated and focused on your goals.

Overcoming Plateaus

Tip 98: Take a break: Sometimes, taking a short break from training can help you come back refreshed and re-energized. Don't be afraid to take a few days off if you need it.

Taking a break from training can be an important part of any cross country running routine. Rest days and breaks can help prevent burnout and injury and allow your body to recover and rebuild. Here are some tips for taking a break from training:

First, listen to your body. If you're feeling tired, run-down, or experiencing any pain or discomfort, it may be a sign that you need a break. It's important to pay attention to your body's signals and take time off when you need it.

Second, plan your break in advance. Consider taking a few days off after a particularly intense training cycle or race, or schedule regular rest days into your weekly routine.

Third, stay active during your break, but in a less intense way. This could mean going for a walk or a light jog, doing some yoga or stretching, or trying out a new form of cross-training like swimming or cycling.

Fourth, use your break as an opportunity to focus on recovery. This could mean getting enough sleep, eating a nutritious diet, and incorporating foam rolling or other recovery techniques into your routine.

Fifth, stay mentally engaged with your training during your break. Read about cross country running, watch videos of races or workouts or set goals for your next training cycle.

Finally, ease back into training gradually after your break. Don't jump back into your regular routine at full speed right away. Instead, start with shorter, easier runs and gradually increase your distance and intensity over time.

In summary, taking a break from training can be an important part of any cross country running routine. By listening to your body, planning your break in advance, staying active in a less intense way, focusing on recovery, staying mentally engaged with your training, and easing back into training gradually, you can come back refreshed and re-energized, ready to tackle your next challenge.

Tip 99: Change up your routine: If you've hit a plateau in your training, it might be time to switch things up. Try a new workout, change your running route, or mix up your cross-training.

If you've been following the same cross country running routine for a while and are no longer seeing improvements, it may be time to change things up. Here are some tips for how to do that:

First, try a new workout. Incorporating different types of workouts, such as hill repeats, tempo runs, or interval training, can challenge your body in new ways and help you break through a plateau.

Second, change your running route. Running the same route day after day can become monotonous, so switch up your scenery and explore new trails or paths. This can also help you avoid overuse injuries caused by running on the same surface too often.

Third, mix up your cross-training. Try new forms of cross-training, such as swimming, cycling, or weightlifting, to target different muscles and improve your overall fitness.

Fourth, adjust your training schedule. If you usually run in the morning, try running in the afternoon or evening instead. Changing up the time of day can help you break out of a rut and feel more energized during your runs.

Fifth, focus on your mental game. Sometimes a plateau can be caused by a lack of motivation or focus. Work on developing mental toughness, setting goals, and visualizing success to help you push through tough workouts and see improvements in your performance.

Finally, consider working with a coach or joining a running group to get new ideas and support. They can provide guidance on how to adjust your training and offer accountability to help you stick to your new routine.

In summary, changing up your cross country running routine can help you break through plateaus and see new improvements in your performance. By trying new workouts, changing your running route, mixing up your cross-training, adjusting your training schedule, focusing on your mental game, and seeking support from others, you can keep your training fresh and challenging.

Tip 100: Work on your mental game: Sometimes, the biggest obstacle to progress is mental. Work on developing a positive attitude and visualization techniques to help you push through difficult workouts and plateaus.

Cross country running is not just about physical strength and endurance but also about mental toughness. Developing a positive attitude and visualization techniques can help you push through difficult workouts and break through plateaus. Here are some tips for working on your mental game:

First, practice positive self-talk. Instead of focusing on negative thoughts or doubts about your abilities, train yourself to think positively. Use affirmations, such as "I am strong" or "I can do this," to boost your confidence and motivation.

Second, use visualization techniques. Close your eyes and visualize yourself running with ease, feeling strong and confident. Picture yourself achieving your goals, whether it's finishing a race or hitting a new personal record. This technique can help you stay motivated and focused during tough workouts.

Third, set realistic goals. Having clear and achievable goals can help you stay focused and motivated. Make sure to set both short-term and long-term goals and track your progress along the way.

Fourth, celebrate your successes. Take time to acknowledge your achievements and celebrate your progress. This can help boost your confidence and keep you motivated to keep going.

Finally, practice mindfulness techniques. Incorporate meditation or breathing exercises into your routine to help you stay calm and focused during stressful situations. This can also help you stay present and focused during your runs.

In summary, working on your mental game is just as important as physical training when it comes to cross country running. By practicing positive self-talk, visualization techniques, goal-setting, celebrating successes, and mindfulness techniques, you can develop the mental toughness needed to push through difficult workouts and plateaus.

Tip 101: Incorporate rest days: Rest and recovery are just as important as training. Make sure to schedule regular rest days and listen to your body if you need to take an extra day off.

Incorporating rest days into your training is crucial for preventing injury and promoting recovery. Rest allows your muscles and joints to repair and rebuild after the stress of training. Here are some tips for incorporating rest days into your training routine:

First, schedule regular rest days. Plan your training schedule with at least one or two rest days each week. These rest days can be active rest days, where you engage in low-impact activities like walking or yoga, or complete rest days, where you avoid any physical activity.

Second, listen to your body. If you feel tired or sore, take an extra rest day or modify your workout. Pushing through fatigue or pain can lead to injury or burnout. Your body will tell you when it needs rest, so pay attention to how you feel.

Third, use rest days for recovery. Incorporate activities that promote recovery on your rest days, such as foam rolling, stretching, or getting a massage. These activities can help alleviate soreness and improve mobility.

Fourth, stay active on rest days. Engage in low-impact activities like walking or swimming to keep your body moving and promote circulation. This can also help you mentally recharge and destress.

In summary, incorporating regular rest days into your training routine is essential for preventing injury and promoting recovery. Listen to your body, use rest days for recovery, and stay active in low-impact ways to maintain your fitness and overall health.

Chapter Review

- Mix up your routes to keep things interesting and prevent monotony in your training.

- Incorporate different types of workouts, such as hill repeats, tempo runs, and interval training, to challenge your body in different ways and improve your overall fitness.
- Keep a training log to track your progress, stay motivated, and celebrate your accomplishments.
- Join a running club or find a running buddy to provide accountability, support, and motivation.
- Set realistic goals, take rest days, and work on your mental game to overcome plateaus and make progress in your training.

About the Author

Elliott Redcay is a passionate and dedicated cross country runner with a wealth of experience in the sport. He has competed at the high school level and has helped coach and train runners of all ages and skill levels. In just one season, he was able to drop his 5k time from 19 minutes to an impressive 16:43. With his extensive knowledge and expertise, Elliott has created a comprehensive and practical guide to help others achieve their own running goals. His tips and strategies are based on personal experience and proven training methods, making him a trusted source for anyone looking to improve their cross country running performance.

HowExpert publishes how to guides on all topics from A to Z by everyday experts. Visit HowExpert.com to learn more.

About the Publisher

Byungjoon "BJ" Min / 민병준 is a Korean American author, publisher, entrepreneur, and founder of HowExpert. He started off as a once broke convenience store clerk to eventually becoming a fulltime internet marketer and finding his niche in publishing. The mission of HowExpert is to discover, empower, and maximize everyday people's talents to ultimately make a positive impact in the world for all topics from A to Z. Visit BJMin.com and HowExpert.com to learn more. John 3:16

Recommended Resources

- HowExpert.com – How To Guides on All Topics from A to Z by Everyday Experts.
- HowExpert.com/free – Free HowExpert Email Newsletter.
- HowExpert.com/books – HowExpert Books
- HowExpert.com/courses – HowExpert Courses
- HowExpert.com/clothing – HowExpert Clothing
- HowExpert.com/membership – HowExpert Membership Site
- HowExpert.com/affiliates – HowExpert Affiliate Program
- HowExpert.com/jobs – HowExpert Jobs
- HowExpert.com/writers – Write About Your #1 Passion/Knowledge/Expertise & Become a HowExpert Author.
- HowExpert.com/resources – Additional HowExpert Recommended Resources
- YouTube.com/HowExpert – Subscribe to HowExpert YouTube.
- Instagram.com/HowExpert – Follow HowExpert on Instagram.
- Facebook.com/HowExpert – Follow HowExpert on Facebook.
- TikTok.com/@HowExpert – Follow HowExpert on TikTok.

Made in United States
Cleveland, OH
01 May 2025

16544495R00076